Hunting Booger Bottom

Hunting Booger Bottom

Life Lessons from the Field

Michael Waddell

with

Mike Schoby

HARPER LUXE

An Imprint of HarperCollinsPublishers

HarperCollins books may be purchased for educational, business, or sales promotional use. For information please write: Special Markets Department, HarperCollins Publishers, 10 East 53rd Street, New York, NY 10022.

All photos courtesy of the author.

FIRST HARPERLUXE EDITION

HarperLuxe™ is a trademark of HarperCollins Publishers

Library of Congress Cataloging-in-Publication Data is available upon request.

ISBN: 978-0-06-194600-4

10 11 12 13 14   ID/OPM 10 9 8 7 6 5 4 3 2 1

Contents

Foreword

MICHAEL WADDELL, MY BLOODBROTHER

The ultimate compliment one can give to another is to say that they are "grounded." That means they are stable, reliable, trustworthy, sensible, and solidly in the asset column of life, beaming with positive energy and aliveness. The term means exactly what it says: of the ground, connected to the good Mother Earth, functioning in harmony and at one with our surroundings. My life has been immeasurably enriched by the long list of great men with whom I have shared spiritual campfires for sixty years, so far. Men like Fred Bear, the great conservation visionary who baptized an entire generation of American families in the soul-cleansing world of hands-on resource stewardship via the mystical flights of our aboriginal arrows.

A heart-, body-, and soul-warming campfire brings out one's true colors. Sitting together by a campfire allows deep, powerful relationships to form. I think of my mother and father, brothers and sister, wife, children, and grandchildren first and foremost. My aunts and uncles, cousins and bandmates are with me by the fire also. So are Bob Foulkrod, Dick Mauch, Ward Parker, Rick Perry, Scott Young, Jim Lawson, Paul Wilson, Marv Leslie, Bob Blevins, Steve, Gary, and Mike Sims, George Nicholls, Randy Rifenburg, Michael Waddell, and many, many more.

Michael Waddell is my BloodBrother. It wouldn't matter when or where we shared these fires, we would still connect, whether it was the year one or 2010. Michael is the real McCoy. Down-to-earth, clever, genuine, well-grounded, funny as all hell, kind, generous, decent, and surely one of the best natural hunters and woodsmen I have ever grilled a sacred backstrap with. A natural born predator of the highest order, Michael is truly a master bowhunter, rifleman, shotgunner, game-caller, and instinctive naturalist who stands with the best that have ever lived. I can honestly say that he ranks right up there with what legend makes of Davy Crockett and Daniel Boone. If I were to be stranded on a jungle island, I am confident that I would not sacrifice any quality of life if Michael were there with me. I know that we would eat well and laugh heartily.

Michael has risen to a well-earned position of leadership in the world of hunting, fishing, and all things

American-outdoor-family-fun. Some would use the term "celebrity," but I would not. Celebrity is too shallow. "Leadership" better identifies his influential role in recruiting new sporters into the glorious world of hands-on conservation environmentalism and the exciting shooting-sports disciplines. With his sincere enthusiasm and contagious, believable authenticity, Michael never apologizes but rather promotes and celebrates this last, perfect, values-based respect for God's magical natural creation of tooth, fang, and claw. To watch Michael call in a cagey old long-beard tom turkey or spirit-rattling bull elk is to witness sheer poetry in motion. His hunting moves are as graceful as a hungry lion stalking and killing its prey, like a life-and-death ballet.

Buy this book for everybody you know, for the life that Michael Waddell lives is not only available to every man, woman, and child in the Free World, but will bring an immediate quality-of-life upgrade as the healing powers of nature permeate your very being. Be like Mike and celebrate this fascinating, thrilling Spirit of the Wild with all the gusto you can summon. Live life to the fullest and get grounded ASAP. It will cleanse the soul.

TED NUGENT

A BOY FROM BOOGER BOTTOM

I grew up in a little area of Georgia called Booger Bottom. You won't likely pass any road signs saying Booger Bottom. There ain't no stores, or stop lights neither. You probably won't find it on any map, but it's there all the same, just stop and ask somebody. They'll point you in the right direction.

Booger Bottom is located down among the crick bottoms and the moss-covered oak groves. There are a few old farmsteads left over from the old days, and some are still planting row crops in the red dirt. Booger Bottom is a small community made up of very country, very rural people. It was no secret that a lot of moonshine was made back in those hollows along the cricks. I am often asked where the name "Booger Bottom" comes from, and rightly, I really don't know. If you ask some of the locals, they say it had to do with the federal agents who came in and busted up moonshine liquor stills during the Prohibition (federal agents were often called boogers in parts of the South); others claim the area was inhabited by a booger—a kind of animal that supposedly looked like a panther mixed with a rabid wild dog. If you talk to some of the older folks they all can tell you of their stepbrother's cousin's friend who ran across the beast one night walking home. Some stories go all the way back to the FDR days, when he came into Warm Springs for treatment of his polio. Evidently the federal agents had to walk from Warm Springs back through this here valley. Every time they did, something would get after them, running in the bushes beside them, which they referred to as a booger, or spook.

Hunting has been part of my life for as long as I can recall. People often ask why I hunt, and I really don't have much of an answer, as I can't imagine life without it. I guess the simple answer is, because hunting is me. It is in my blood, it is in my culture, and it is in my family. Hunting comprises my earliest recollections of my dad and my uncle Morgan Whitaker. They hunted not just as a pastime or part-time recreation, but as a full-time obsession. It was their lifestyle—and our family's main source of food.

I was probably around nine when I realized my dad hunted just because he liked to. Sure, we needed the meat, but he was a sport hunter all the same. Not in the negative sense associated with the term today, but in its true sense as in sportsman, as a gentleman. He just simply enjoyed being afield after game.

My father worked anywhere from fifty to sixty hours a week, Monday through Friday, so Saturday and Sunday were dedicated to hunting. Eventually this caused a rub between him and Mom 'cause he was so dedicated and so on fire to go hunting at the drop of a hat. One time in particular my mom said, "If I come home and see your gun gone, then I know your hunting means more to you than me."

When I came home from school I was praying that Dad's gun would be in the cabinet and he would be there waiting, cleaning up around the house, maybe with some roses on the table, but when I walked through that door that cold November afternoon, there was no worn 742 Remington Woodsmaster in the cabinet and no Dad. Even though I hoped he would be there, I knew deep down that he wouldn't be. At that time I hadn't started to hunt yet, but I knew enough from listening to him and Uncle Morgan talk to know that the rut was on, and when the temperature drops, it was the best time to be in the woods. I knew Dad wouldn't be home before I walked in the door.

My momma was furious. She started crying and saying "I can't believe he went hunting," over and over.

Somehow I knew how important it was for my dad, so I immediately went on the defensive for him. "Mom, the rut is on. Daddy has been working hard, this is something he enjoys." I realized right then and there that hunting invoked some serious passion, because there was something about hunting that pushed my dad to a point he could not return from. Whether it was competitive—to kill a big buck—or whether it was just him being alone out there in the stand, away from everything—just him and nature and his ability to go one-on-one with an animal—it all blended together. I learned then that hunting was an emotional disease, something akin to an addiction. I knew that my dad loved my mom and his family, but there was nothing that could keep him from the woods that cold November day.

As I got older and drawn to hunting like my father, Booger Bottom became my playground, my school, and my life, and I have never left it. I have traveled literally around the world and seen some amazing places. I have hunted Cape buffalo with natives in Africa, ridden horses for moose in Alaska, and hiked over the Rocky Mountains more times than my aching body cares to remember. But Booger Bottom still calls to me.

The most memorable and cherished hunts I have ever had were with my father. While I have said many times that the kill is why I hunt, equally important to me is sharing the kill with a family member. As far as hunting goes, no one has ever been more important in my life than my papa.

It was Papa and Uncle Morgan that really got me into the outdoors and introduced me to the sport. And it was my papa who encouraged me to get involved in the industry through turkey-calling competitions, which somehow turned into a career. He also taught me a solid work ethic at an early age, which has served me well in whatever I have done throughout life, so when I get a chance to just hunt, without worrying about cameras, I always choose to spend that time with him.

Family is the most important thing in my life, and that was instilled in me from an early age. To understand my passion for family, one has to understand my upbringing and my relationship with my father.

We had it good when I was a kid—we weren't rich, mind you, but we never wanted for anything, and my dad worked hard every day. We never went without.

I think the reason he worked so hard to provide for his family was because he never had anything growing up. He'd had a pretty tough childhood. He was from a divorced family. He had a ninth-grade education (he recalls getting tired of shaving for school in the ninth grade, so instead of shaving he just quit school and started working in construction). He bounced around from Georgia to Alabama to Florida to California. All that moving around was with an abusive stepfather. It was a pretty tough, traumatic childhood.

My father has told me the best thing he ever got was a bicycle for Christmas one year. Well, not exactly a whole bicycle, more like a share in a bicycle. Along with him, his two brothers and his older sister got that single bicycle to share. While it wasn't as good as each one of them having a bike, it was still a bike and their pride and joy. Well, that February they were out in the yard, changing a tire on it, when a Western Auto truck came pulling up in the drive. A guy got out, didn't say a word. He just grabbed the bike and tossed it in the truck and drove off. Their bike had just got repo'd. Evidently Santa Claus hadn't paid the bill.

But from all those traumatic experiences he'd faced as a child, rather than becoming a victim as an adult, he used his "victimization" as an opportunity. It was his chance to fix it with his own family.

The biggest thing he always did was to give back to me. Not only was he always there for football and baseball practice, but the number-one thing we enjoyed together from my young age was hunting. He always was, and always will be, my hero. Not because he was well educated. Not because he was a rich man, an entrepreneur, a famous athlete, or a business tycoon. The reason he's my hero is because of what he stood for and his outlook on life. His theory was: work hard, respect others, do unto others as you would have them do unto you, and keep your priorities straight when it comes to your family.

He lived his childhood through me and tried to provide for me the things he never had as a kid. The biggest thing he tried to create was that bond between father and son that he never had with his dad.

My mother's influence was equally important, even if her time with us was shorter.

I remember it like it was yesterday, we were sitting around the dinner table, just getting ready to eat one of my mother's phenomenal meals, when Dad looked across the table at her and said, "Woman, what's that bruise on your neck? Looks like a hickey—you been out running around on me?" He said it with a grin. Mom said, "I know, it just came up. In fact, I have had several of them, and have been so weak lately." Dad quit grinning and pulling her leg and said in a serious tone, "Well, you better go see the doctor, then."

It wasn't long after that Mom went to the doctor. What she learned shocked us all to the core. She had leukemia. She was thirty-four years old. She had me, my adopted sister, and six foster kids she had taken under her wing. In her mind, she was just too busy to have a life-threatening disease. "Edwin," she told my dad, "don't you worry about it. I'm not worried, I'll beat this thing in no time."

And she really did believe it, too. She was tough and there was not a doubt in her mind that she would whip leukemia. Well, it proved tougher than she had thought. Mom went in for procedure after procedure, until the point came where she pretty much lived in the hospital. Dad and I were essentially living in a house that now felt very empty indeed, doing whatever we could to cope with the situation, the unknown, and the fear.

During Mom's sickness, a local catfish farm donated a bunch of their fish to have a catfish fry to raise money for her hospital bills. So Daddy and I went over to help seine the lake to get the catfish. We worked hard all night, skinning and cutting up fish. We got a few hours' sleep and got up the next morning after cleaning catfish all night. Our hands were all cut up from them catfish finning us, and we were covered in catfish slime. The morning dawned cold and we headed to the stands. I didn't get anything that morning, but Dad killed a big old doe. While it was "just a doe," seeing the glimmer in my daddy's eye meant so much to me, just to know that we would always have this. It was just him and me out in the middle of the woods, loading that doe up on the back of the truck. The silence driving back was overwhelming. We were tired from trying to raise money, both of us worried for Momma, but the peace of that hunt helped the healing process. That hunt made me realize that everything was going to be all right, no matter what happened, no matter what the outcome was, no matter what our finances were. We would still have hunting to tie us together, and that was something that nobody could take away from us.

Late winter turned into spring, and spring rolled around into summer, and by June, Mom knew she wasn't going to win this fight, so they let her come home to be with her family. She died at home with us shortly thereafter. I was sixteen.

Now Dad was alone. He had six foster kids, my sister, and me to raise by himself. He was flat broke from paying for Momma's medical bills. Well, the first thing that happened was that Child Protective Services came in and removed the foster children. In their eyes, what business did a broke, single dad have raising two kids (me and my sister), much less six other kids? So now our bulging happy house that Mom had filled with love, cooking, and children was lonely and quiet and just filled with Daddy, me, and my sister. While we had each other, which is the reason for our tight bond today, one of our biggest and most immediate problems was what were we going to eat.

In today's world of microwavable everything, eating is often taken for granted. But after the dishes that people brought over for us ran out and we got tired of McDonald's, we had to give some serious consideration to providing for ourselves. My mom was the best cook on earth. When she was alive, we never worried about anything. Every night there was a major home-cooked meal on the table. On Saturdays and Sundays there were always big breakfasts and lunches and a big supper. Because of this, I was always a fat little kid. It is easy to see my mom's passing away just by looking at my photos. I went from being a fat little kid to nearly scrawny in a pretty short time. I remember shortly after all this happened that Dad and I were sitting on the couch, and Dad turned to me and said, "What we gonna eat?" It just hit us. Here we were, on our own, completely independent. Dad can build the Empire State Building with a claw hammer, sixteen-penny nails, a little bit of wood, and a Skil saw, but this cooking issue had us stumped. We were broke and we really had no idea how to cook much of anything. The one thing Pa and I could do was grow tomatoes and Silver Queen corn in our vegetable garden, and we were smart enough to boil water for the corn and eat the 'maters raw.

Around that time, I started dating girls, and I had this cute little blonde girlfriend. One day Dad said, "Why don't you bring your date over and I'll cook us a little supper." So I told the girl, "If you don't mind, would you like to come over for dinner tonight, my dad would like to meet ya."

So I brought Lori (who later turned out to be my first wife) over to the house. After introductions were made, we sat down at the dinner table and Daddy came out with this huge stainless-steel pot, like a deep-fryer for turkeys. He set it on the table and placed a little squeeze bottle of Country Crock butter with salt and pepper alongside it with some dinner rolls he made.

He looked up over the pot at Lori and said, "Well, tonight we're eating corn."

She was great about it. She didn't act like anything was weird about it or nothing. So all of us dug in and sat around, eating corn on the cob, four or five ears apiece, and that was supper. That became the standard dinner at the Waddell house. We knew how to grow corn, could shuck some ears and boil it. Many a night Daddy and I would sit down and eat five, maybe six ears of corn apiece and nothing else.

After several weeks of our new diet I broke out in horrible red spots all across my face. At first I thought it was acne, but it turned into more of a rash, so I decided to go to the doctor. The doc in town looked at it and asked me if I had changed soap, shampoo, hair conditioner, or any laundry detergent. When I said no to all of the above, he then asked if I had been eating anything different lately, especially anything with high acid content.

"Well, actually, yeah, Doc, I have changed my diet and have been eating a lot of 'maters and corn lately."

"How many tomatoes have you been eating?"

"Oh, I don't know, I'd guess around eight or nine a day."

The doctor smiled, shook his head while chuckling, and said, "Well, there's your problem, quit eating so many tomatoes."

From my humble begins, I have been so blessed with the opportunities I have had and the goals I have achieved, all of it so far beyond my wildest dreams growing up in Booger Bottom. I know my daddy is proud of me and my accomplishments, but he is not the kind to ever praise me or tell me directly. But as soon as I am out of the room, he is constantly telling everyone how "great" I am to the point that it is pathetic. Even with his braggin' on me, I am very conscious of the fact that Dad is me and I am Dad. We are one and the same.

With my father, what you see is what you get. There are no false trappings or put-on appearances. Good, bad, or ugly, with us you get everything at face value. The Waddell clan's Achilles' heel is probably language. I say that because my dad is not someone who can sit there and use big words—or, to put it another way, he definitely doesn't use a thesaurus much. But just 'cause he messes big words up now and again, that don't stop him from giving them a try. I am not just poking fun at my pa either here, as I stumble my share when I try to use big words. I mess them up as well.

But it doesn't matter to either one of us. I am not a grammar teacher. I am somebody who represents a culture of people who make mistakes. Even the most educated person in the world makes mistakes in one form or another—it just so happens in my family it's words. So no matter how many words my dad messes up, I am always proud to have him around.

But Daddy is so candid and honest with everyone he meets that sometimes you have to watch out, as he will just shoot from the hip and say what is on his mind. He provides a bit of honesty and humbleness that is so missing in today's world. I wish I could take him to every meeting with me. As anyone who meets him will tell ya, he is as real as the day is long. There is no b.s., just true sincerity.

Now that I am a father and I better understand all the gifts of life he has given me, there is not a day that goes by when I don't have a desire to give something back to him. Now, one thing we have talked about since I was a kid was elk hunting. He has always wanted to kill an elk. But as much as he wants to do it, he is just that type of guy who would always talk about it but die never having taken the time or effort to go out West and give it a try. At home he's had lots of success with turkey and deer. But travel out of state to go hunting? Not him.

So in the past few years it's been my mission to make sure that Dad gets the opportunity to come to full draw on an elk. No matter what it costs me, no matter what I have to do, no matter where we have to go, I am going to make sure it happens.

In that light, in 2006 we hunted out in New Mexico. We hunted an unbelievable spot in the Gila National Forest, during the middle of the rut. While we hunted hard for seven days, we just could never close the coffin on a bull. We heard bulls every day, but since Daddy is a bit hard of hearing, he didn't hear as many as everyone else did . . . but he still had a great time. This year I have a hunt lined up in Colorado for Daddy and me to try and get one.

As much as the industry has given to me, I think he has given me even more. He gave me my foundation. He gave me my understanding of who I am, where I come from, and where I am going. As I have achieved success in life and in the hunting industry, I have been asked many times, can I remain grounded, can I remain true to my roots and keep my feet on solid ground. As long as I have my dad, it is easy to stay grounded. I owe him a lot for that. There ain't anything guaranteed in life, other than that it'll end one day, so you can't take things for granted and put things off from year to year. As soon as you can make something happen, you need to make it happen. So as far as hunting with my dad goes, every chance I can make it happen, I do.

Because of my job I am out of state a lot and don't get the chance to hunt with him as much as I'd like, but one thing I did make a commitment to do was to always hunt the family ground with my dad opening day of turkey season. And we have never missed an opening day since I was fourteen years old. Though it has changed somewhat. Now it is no longer Dad and me carrying guns, trying to kill gobblers. Now we are out there acting like professional guides for my two boys. I had a chance to see my son Mason at seven years old kill his first turkey in the same area I killed my first turkey when Dad and I were learning to hunt turkeys together back when I was thirteen. What was even more special was that he was sitting between his grandpa's legs when he pulled the trigger.

When I saw the twinkle in my boy's eyes as he looked at me, and my papa, and his first turkey, I knew we'd just created another boy from Booger Bottom. Hopefully his momma will understand when she comes home and both of our guns are missing from the cabinet.

2

THE BIG BUCK OF MERIWETHER COUNTY

In Georgia, hunting, fishing, and the outdoors are as ingrained in our culture as rodeo is out West, or soccer in many other countries. But in Georgia, it's funny. It seems like kids come right off breast milk, get a gun, head to the woods, and start hunting. I was no different. Booger Bottom had plenty of places to hunt for squirrels and rabbits, and, brother, let me tell you, I simply wore out the small-game population with my .22 by the time I was old enough to read. But as much as I loved hunting the smaller stuff around the farm, I was always looking for the next adventure, and the biggest adventure you could have in Georgia was deer hunting. By the time I was old enough to hunt white-tails, it was all I could think about.

Some hunters like to defend the sport by arguing that it's all about game management. I have a huge problem with the term "harvesting" animals. Both the term and the concept. The term in itself tries to soften the effect of what we really mean, which is kill. If we mean kill, we should say "kill." But more important than the semantics is the justification. Hunters certainly do have to play a role in today's society as game managers. But wildlife management is not why we hunt. Sure, we need to take care of the wildlife, but we hunt because we love it. Let's not kid ourselves. The worst thing that could ever happen for hunters is that we no longer need to manage wildlife for their own well-being. If a day came when either native predators expanded their range to such an extent that they were keeping deer and elk in check (such as in the West, where wolf and cougar numbers are exploding right now) then hunters will have lost that justification. We need to be honest with people, and let them know that we hunt because we love to hunt.

When I turned eleven, Daddy deemed me old enough to hunt deer. Today times are a bit different than they were back then. Now many fathers buy a specific rifle for their young-uns to get started deer hunting with. Oftentimes this may be a single-shot or a bolt-action in a smaller caliber like .243 Winchester or .25-06. But not my dad. My first gun was my dad's old Remington

742 Woodsmaster, which is a semiautomatic chambered in .30-06. I practiced shooting with it out in the backyard, and it had a pretty good bit of recoil, but I got used to it and could manage to hit the bull's-eye pretty good even though the stock was a bit long for me. I realized early on that living in the country you had to be tough, and if you wanted to go hunting you had to be even tougher, so I never complained, as I surely didn't want to have to wait another year to get bigger before I could go on the annual deer hunt.

After what seemed like weeks of practicing and an eternity of sleepless nights spent staring at the ceiling, thinking of big bucks behind every tree, opening morning finally arrived. While I always had a tough time getting up for school, I believe I was up before my father and was dressed and ready to go well before light. My father and I left the house on foot and headed to the back of our property, what's left of the old Waddell farm. It's a beautiful mix of rolling hills covered with hardwoods and crop fields. We snuck through the woods in the dark to get to our tree stands. It was still a piece before first light cracked the eastern sky when my dad boosted me into a homemade wooden stand up in this big ole pine.

Before he left he said, "Look, you know how to shoot, and I showed you how to be safe. Remember your instructions. If you see anything with horns on it, it's a buck and it's legal to kill." With that brief instruction, he disappeared into the predawn gloom. In retrospect, I don't know if I was even legal to be up in that tree without an adult, but at the same time I was from Booger Bottom . . . it wasn't like we saw law much.

Back in those days Georgia consisted of a lot of row crop—corn and beans, mainly. My stand was looking over a cut cornfield, but it hadn't all been cut. There was still a little bit of standing corn. I had barely got settled and the day had just broke enough to see when I looked out in the field, and about 70 yards away I noticed this deer standing there, feeding in the standing corn. I got to looking closer and I could see small spikes breaking through this deer's head. Now keep in mind, my daddy had left the stand location no more than ten minutes before. I was as green as a gourd to deer hunting and here I am with a deer in front me—a legal buck, no less!

The Woodsmaster was equipped with an old Bushnell scope with those aluminum over and under rings, the kind where you can see through the scope but also look underneath it at the iron sights. My father's instructions on the fine art of shooting deer, while brief, ran in my head. "Take the first shot through the scope 'cause you have 3-to-9 magnification. If you shoot and he starts running, come down to those iron sights and give him hell. You got four more bullets in the clip." And my dad clearly showed me how to load that 742, putting four in the clip, cycling the action, then putting another in the clip, so I had a total of five shots. Perfect for a trigger-happy boy of eleven. His final words of wisdom were: "Always make sure you got your second clip handy."

This overgrown button head was feeding his way through the corn, and I decided to shoot him. I aimed down and found him in those iron sights first, then went up and found him in that ole 3-to-9, which of course I had cranked all the way up to 9 power.

I slowly squeezed the trigger. The rifle roared and bucked, but I never felt the recoil. When I looked up that buck was in the dirt! My first year of deer hunting, the first morning, not ten minutes into the season, and my first deer was dead. It seemed like the sound had barely quit echoing through the woods when my dad was at the base of my tree.

He looked up at me and said, "Did you get you one?"

"Yes sir, he is laying right there," I said, pointing out into the field.

My dad gave me a thumbs-up, smiled, pumped his fist, and walked out to confirm the kill.

When he returned, he said, "Good deal, boy, ya gotcha a spike. Sit tight. I'm going to go down to the island stand and hunt for a bit, so just stay up there and chill out." With that he walked off.

No more than five minutes after he left the second time I look up, and here's another deer standing at the edge of the field. It's another spike, except this one had about three or four more inches of antler sticking up.

Well, my dad had never talked about limits or anything, he just said "Sit tight." He didn't say don't shoot any more deer. The way I looked at it was, I'd taken one shot out of a clip of five. I still had four more bullets, and another clip in my pocket, so I had plenty of ammo.

So I bore down again, and repeated the sighting process just like with the first buck and took a shot. I don't know if I hit him or not, but he took off running toward me so I proceeded to shoot two more times using the iron sights just like I was taught. He piled up in the cornfield not far from the first buck. It turned out I ended up hitting him with two out of the three shots. All of this within maybe twenty minutes of daybreak on my first deer hunt.

So now I have two deer down and I am pumped. Both of 'em were spikes, but I didn't care, they were bucks. Trophies didn't matter much to anyone in our neck of the woods back then. We weren't trophy hunters, we were just hunters. All deer ate the same to us.

Once again my dad comes walking back to my stand. He hasn't even gotten a chance to get up in his stand yet. Instead of hollering up from the base of the tree, this time he climbs up to my stand and says with a grave look on his face, "Are you okay?"

It was obvious he thought I had accidentally discharged my rifle.

With a grin I said, "Yeah, Daddy, I'm fine! I just shot another one!"

"You shot another one?" he said in disbelief.

He then looked out into the field and saw the second spike and said, "Well, I wished you wouldn't have shot another small deer."

Of course he had never even talked about what was small and what was big, and to me a deer was just a deer, if it was brown it was down. I was just excited about being up there in the tree, giving out parking tickets. To me a deer was the same as a squirrel. I just knew we hunted them and I just closed two coffins.

So, shaking his head, Dad began to climb back down the tree. He left me with the final instructions of "Chill out and let your dad have a chance to go hunt. I am going to walk back down to the island stand. I am going to hunt about two hours, then I'll come back and get ya. Just stay warm and be safe. I'll be back."

Dad no more than left again and almost got to his stand, which wasn't much more than a fifteen-minute walk, and I looked to the corner of the field and out pops a doe. She was looking behind her. Since I only had about fifteen minutes of experience under my deer-hunting belt, I knew nothing about deer habits, the rut, or anything else.

But, looking back, it was around the end of the first week of November, which was right around the peak of the rut, which is a prime time for catching trophy bucks chasing does, especially when the weather gets cooler, which it had that week.

Before I could think much more about it, all of a sudden she took off trotting across the field, and when I looked back to where she had been all I saw was a big rack sticking out of the corner of the field.

Dad's last instructions ran through my mind. All he had said was "chill out, be safe, and stay warm," but at the same time he never unloaded my gun, nor did he specifically say, "Don't shoot any more deer."

It was no more than a few seconds from the time I saw the rack until this big buck stepped out. He was as big as any of the deer my dad had on the wall. "Oh my gawd," I muttered. I can remember buck fever just overcoming me, freaking me out. He was breathing smoke 'cause it was cold out, with a hard frost on the ground. I forgot everything Dad said about sitting tight and chilling out. I was fidgeting and as high-strung as you could get! All I knew was there was a big buck in front of me and hopefully I still had enough parking tickets left in my gun that I could issue him one.

So once again I found this buck with my iron sights first, then came up on the scope. Right when I saw hair in the crosshairs I pulled the trigger. I didn't have a clue if I hit him or not, all I knew is I pulled the trigger when I had hair in the scope. The deer took off running and made a little U-turn in the field and headed back into the woods. Since he didn't drop in sight like the two spikes, I was totally convinced I'd missed him.

This time my dad is 100 percent sure I just had a hunting accident. He literally came running back up to my stand and practically yelled, "What are you doing? Are you okay?"

With an even wider grin I said, "Daddy, I shot another one!"

"I told you not to shoot any more deer!"

"No, Daddy, you told me to be safe and stay warm and chill out, you never said anything about not shooting."

I crawled down the tree, and he said, "What were you shooting at?" still a bit upset.

"I was shooting at one as big as what you got on the wall."

With a curious smile he replied, "How big was he?"

My tongue was moving faster than my thoughts, which rambled out in one long uninterrupted sentence: "I don't know he just had a big rack with a big body and he followed a doe out and I shot at him but I missed him."

"Well, show me where he was standing."

So we walked over to the edge of the cut corn and I showed him where the deer was at when I shot. You could clearly see the fresh tracks and where the frost had been disturbed.

"Yeah, that's a big ole buck all right. Whew . . . look at the track on him," Dad said, with a hint of surprise and appreciation.

You could see where he was running clearly in the fresh dirt and frost, so we followed the track about twenty yards, and I will never forget it, there was a huge spot of blood on a white rock, and Daddy said, "Well, you hit him."

We found a little more blood and then the next thing I know we hit the woods line and there was so much blood there, it was like it was poured out of a bucket. Dad said with confidence, "You got him. I don't know where he is, but you got him."

So we got down there in the woods, and sure enough there he was, a big old buck laying dead just inside the woods line. He had five points on one side and on the other side he had a big screwed-up nontypical rack. And while the rack was amazing, the body size of this deer was simply enormous.

When we got back to the house, Uncle Morgan went crazy. After looking him over, he said, "This buck is big enough he could win the local big buck contest." Now, growing up in Georgia, we never knew anything about Boone and Crockett scoring, so every big buck contest was based totally on the field-dressed weight of the deer.

We had an old Chevy pickup truck and we loaded all them deer up and took them to the Big Buck Trading Post in Manchester, Georgia. Soon after we arrived we were the talk of the contest. No one could recall a buck with that big a body coming out of those parts. When we hoisted him up he was as big as he looked: that big ole freak nasty tipped the scales at 197 pounds field dressed and it won the big buck contest. Now keep in mind, those local big buck contests were a big deal in my neck of the woods. The prize was a gift certificate for $700 at the Big Buck Trading Post.

Like every child, I always had more wants than hard cash, so that gift certificate was like the best Christmas present I ever did receive. Every time we went to that store I was always begging my dad for some money to buy me something. Like any kid, I always wanted candy or ice cream, but I had a real sweet tooth for outdoor gear as well. With that $700 gift certificate burning a hole in my pocket, I was suddenly sort of wealthy. It was a feeling I won't ever forget. Now my dad looked like a little young-un, and for the first time I felt like an adult 'cause I was the one doing the buying. It didn't take long and I noticed Daddy was over at the gun counter, purposefully fondling a Ruger Redhawk .44 Magnum.

"Man, that's a nice gun right there now, son," he said, while turning the cylinder. He just kept talking about this gun and fondling it. Even at my young age, I could tell he was not so subtly dropping a hint that he really wanted me to buy it for him.

So I asked him, "Daddy, do you want that gun?"

He replied, "Aw, don't you never mind me—I do like it now, but it's your money. Spend it on what you want."

So I turned around and looked the revolver over. I don't recall exactly how much it was now, four or five hundred dollars at least. I didn't know anything about revolvers, but I did know that Hank Williams, Jr., loved Rugers, so I figured if it was good enough for Hank Williams, Jr., it was good enough for my daddy. So I bought that handgun and a box of bullets and I ended up getting me one of those little Browning breakdown .22 semiautos, a brick of .22 bullets, and two bottles of Tink's No. 69. My dad gave them ten dollars to boot when it was all said and done and we walked out of there like kings.

That was the point when I knew that, just like my daddy, I was hopelessly hooked on hunting, and I had the affliction bad. From that day forward there was never a time unless I was deathly ill and just couldn't get up out of bed that I wasn't always with my dad and Uncle Morgan during deer season. Not only did that create a passion for whitetail hunting, it created a passion for hunting in general and a lifetime bond between my dad and me. From that point on I knew he would be my number-one hunting partner.

3

I'D RATHER BE LUCKY THAN GOOD

We had a lot of wildlife in Booger Bottom. The main species we hunted were whitetails and small game like rabbits and squirrels. It is a common misconception that turkeys simply cover up the South. In my youth, at least around Booger Bottom, there wasn't any turkeys.

I distinctly remember my first encounter with thunder chickens. I was between thirteen and fourteen when Uncle Morgan came by the house sometime in late winter and said, "You are not going to believe what I saw in the back field by the old corner stand" (the same stand where I killed my first deer). I guessed everything from black panthers to anteaters, trying to imagine what he might have seen, only to find out it was wild turkeys. At that time there were very few, if any, turkeys at all in Meriwether County. My elders had never even seen them in their youth—evidently the old Waddell clan before them must have poached them off long before the War of Northern Aggression. The very little I did know about turkeys was that we ate them at Thanksgiving and bought them at the Piggly Wiggly.

Even though my dad and I knew nothing about turkey, we were smart enough to realize turkeys were something else we could hunt. So it didn't take us long after Uncle Morgan's discovery to get the state regulations. We found out that turkey season came on about the third week in March, so we had a little bit of time to prepare. As it turned out, the more time we had to learn about turkeys, the better.

When I say we knew nothing, I mean NOTHING. So Dad and I went to some sporting goods stores and talked to some guys who had killed turkeys, and they filled us in on the basics. Somebody said, "Well, you need to get yourself an owl call." So we went and bought a little ole Ben Lee owl hooter. Somebody else told us we would need a hen call, so we bought a Lynch "Fool Proof" box call. That was it—that was our complete turkey-hunting arsenal. Back then I knew nothing of slate calls, diaphragms, different locator calls—nothing. We had two calls and in our mind we were set! Heck, we didn't even practice with the calls beforehand. We figured we'd learn on the go.

Not really knowing anything about preseason scouting or locating birds on the roost the night before the hunt, we waited until opening morning before heading for the back of the farm. We left well before light and were walking toward the back field, which was about a half mile from our house. When we got to the corner of the field, we saw our old dog following us. Not wanting the dog to follow us around all morning, my dad picked up a rock and threw it at him. He hit the dog square, and the dog tucked his tail and yipped loudly. As luck would have it, that caused a turkey to sound off in the far trees.

We looked at each other, probably the way any two novices look at each other the first time they hear a bird gobble from the roost—we were in shock.

Dad was holding the owl call and I had the directions. Very few people knew he only had a ninth-grade education, but those that did sure knew he wasn't a great reader. I mean, he could read and all, but it's not like he was gonna win no reading contests or anything. We had decided that I was going to read him the instructions on how to call and he was going to try and perform them.

The directions said to try and say, "Who cooks? Who cooks for you all?" but to start with a single, drawn-out "who."

So Daddy let loose a long drawn-out "whooooo" and that old gobbler just hammered back from the trees.

We were awestruck. For as anyone who hunts turkeys knows, hearing a gobbler hammer through the trees on a cool spring morning is pure magic. It will send shivers through your spine and raise goose bumps on your arm, and that first time can never be duplicated. We just stood there in appreciative awe.

We were just so excited that we had turkeys on the property that we just sat there and repeatedly hooted at him. We were as green as a gourd. Instead of using the owl call to just locate the birds and move in to prepare for fly-down, we just kept makin' 'em gobble and gobble.

After probably fifteen minutes of solid owl calling and gobbling, Daddy says, "Well, I reckon we might as well try and call him up."

I had nearly forgot about trying to call one in.

So we eased into the woods and settled down by an old tree. My dad had went and bought a brand-new Remington 870 pump, which he was letting me use. I sat at the base of the tree with that 870 resting over my knee, pointing in the direction of where the gobbles were coming from.

While my main job was to be the trigger man, my other important job was to read Dad the directions.

So I said, "Daddy, try a yelp. A yelp is three strokes on the box call."

So he made three strokes on the box call.

But the turkey didn't gobble.

So I read further. "Try a cluck. A cluck is two to three consecutive notes."

So Daddy did a passable cluck.

The turkey still didn't gobble.

So I read further. "It is good to combine yelps and clucks."

So Daddy combined the yelps and clucks.

And the bird thundered back.

I was shocked. "Gawd, do it some more, Daddy, it's workin' on him."

So Daddy kept calling, and the gobbler kept responding.

I remember there were instructions for a whine and purr, which we tried, but with no practice it didn't sound that good. All of a sudden the turkey just quit gobbling.

After a few minutes of no noise we looked at each other and just figured the show was over.

"Well, that was fun, we'll have to try it again another morning," Daddy said.

But since the weather was nice and we were in no hurry to get back home, we just sat there, enjoying the morning waking up and kinda practicing our calling. We were just goofin' off, being outdoors together. We were being kinda loud and rustling around a bit when all of a sudden a shot rang out way off in the distance, which I guess must have been another turkey hunter.

When that shot rang out our turkey gobbled and he was literally right in front of us just over the ridge and out of sight. Thank God for that shot, as we would have never knew he was there and surely would have spooked him with as much commotion as we were making.

I immediately got my gun ready and Dad made a couple of clucks and about that time the turkey's head popped up over the knob about 35 to 40 yards away, but it disappeared as fast as it had appeared. I was thinking he must have seen us, for I had heard about their phenomenal eyesight, but as it turns out, the bird was just being a turkey, bouncing its head as it walked toward us. When his head came back up the second time I pulled the trigger.

I couldn't have told you anything about that bird before I pulled the trigger. All I knew was that it was a safe shot and that it was a turkey. I never saw a beard or anything, but I *knew* it had to be a big ole gobbler 'cause in my mind that was the one that I heard gobbling and it had a blue and red head. I didn't know if it was a long beard or a jake, which really didn't matter as I didn't know the difference anyways. Well, like my first deer-hunting experience, I have always been blessed with a fair amount of luck. We come to find out it was a new Georgia state record—jake.

But the fact that it was a jake didn't matter one bit. I killed him and I was so pumped I jumped up to go get him. Evidently I must have only got one pellet in him 'cause his head popped up and he started running around. Being young and spry I caught him and had him down, wrasslin' with him, while Daddy was looking for a stick to kill him with. It was a full-on Georgia goat rope trying to kill that bird. We finally got him dispatched, but even later on, under closer inspection, we never did find a pellet in him. I think I just stunned him with the wad or scared him to death. It taught me a life lesson: I'd rather be lucky than good, although you can't ever stop trying your darnedest to be good.

Turkey hunting, or, rather, turkey calling, taught me another lesson: I could make my own luck. I could play a role in finding them, getting close, then coaxing them into range with the right calling. But I also quickly learned that it wasn't as easy as that first one. I went the next two years hunting hard, nearly every day of the season, before I pulled the trigger on a turkey again.

Along the way I learned about all different manners of turkey calls. I got familiar with slate calls, and my all-time favorite call—a diaphragm. I progressed far past the basic clucks and yelps and eventually mastered all forms of turkey conversation. I boned up on their behavior and their habits. In fact, I owe a lot to those tough turkeys of Booger Bottom, as almost every other place I have hunted birds since has not been as difficult. It was through this difficulty that I really learned how to hunt turkeys. Growing up in an area that had lots of birds, or at least easy birds, wouldn't have given me the education I received.

I didn't realize it or understand it then, but the fact that I got really good at my turkey callin' opened doors this boy from Booger Bottom never in his wildest dreams knew existed.

4

STRUTTIN' ON STAGE

After my first, albeit lucky, success with turkeys, I was hooked. All I could think about was getting better with turkey calls. And since there weren't a lot of turkeys around my neck of the woods, there wasn't a whole lot of knowledgeable turkey hunters to learn from. However, there were a few guys in the area who were known as pretty good callers. The two most notable were Ricky Joe Bishop and Mike Middlebrooks. Both of these guys had gotten involved in turkey-calling competitions and both at one time or another had placed in the state competitions. For rural Georgia this was a big deal, akin to being a collegiate wrestler in Ohio or an all-star basketball player in Indiana.

Ricky Joe and Mike at the time were both working on the advisory staff and calling team for Rohm

Brothers game calls, which is owned by Dale and Robby Rohm. As part of their duties they were supposed to videotape turkey kills for a promotional video. So one day they came to my dad, and Mike said, "Hey, I know you all got some pretty good property. Any chance we could do some videoing back there?"

Well, my dad never needed an excuse to go hunting, so he agreed, providing that we accompanied them. The first time Mike came over to hunt, my dad and I took him out ourselves. Now, keep in mind that while we had good property, turkey hunting in that part of the world is always tough. But once again we got lucky. Lo and behold if we didn't kill a turkey—on video, no less.

While I had been practicing nearly daily calling turkeys, I really didn't know if I was good, bad, or just so-so, since there was really no one around to coach me. I just knew that Daddy and I could kill a turkey now and again. But that day was the first time that a competition turkey caller heard me calling.

After we were done hunting, Mike looked at me and he said, "Man, you are one good turkey caller!"

Well, of course I puffed up about as big as a strutting tom, but I didn't really know if he was serious or just pulling my leg. He just kept on and on saying how good I sounded on that mouth diaphragm, and when he left he gave me several Rohm Brothers mouth calls.

His parting words were, "You practice up, as we got a contest coming up in a couple of weeks and you ought to call in it."

So I practiced, practiced, and practiced. I even went over to his house and practiced with him and Ricky Joe. I was getting better and better, but didn't think I was good enough to compete. The day of the contest I got stage fright so bad I totally chickened out and didn't even enter.

Still, I was a big fan of those contests. All youngsters have their idols. Mine weren't rock stars or baseball players. My idols were champion turkey callers. Guys like Billy McCoy, Joe Drake, Paul Butski, and Dick Kirby took center stage over any sports star or even country music artist at that time in my life. I totally respected their ability to call, and I wanted to be just like them in every way. I had them recorded on a tape and I would listen to them over and over and over again on my little tape player in my room and try to mimic the sounds they could make. Then I would go out to local competitions and listen to guys like Eddie Salter, who was another big legend in my book. But I still hadn't worked up enough nerve to enter a contest.

In the meantime, Ricky Joe and Mike had placed third and fourth in the Georgia State competition, as well as in the Appalachia Open. I knew I was around good company. So I started practicing even more.

Since I was hanging around Ricky Joe and Mike, I had the chance to meet Dale Rohm, who gave me ten diaphragms, two slates, and a couple of box calls. I will never forget my dad and me looking at those free calls in amazement. I wasn't looking at them as free calls but as dollar bills. It was just the country redneck way of looking at things. I was like, "Holy cow, he just gave me twenty-five dollars' worth of mouth calls and another forty dollars' of other calls." I remember thinking, "My gawd, that is the most unbelievable gift someone has ever given me." Up to that point I'd never had anything given to me by someone in the hunting industry. When Dale gave them to me, he said, "I am going to give you these calls, boy, but I want you to do something with 'em. You're a good caller, put 'em to good use."

This was when I finally got enough courage to actually enter a competition. Unfortunately the next one up was the Georgia State Championships, of all things. If it hadn't have been for Dale, I wouldn't have entered. It was his gift that gave me the courage to compete, 'cause I felt like I had to—not necessarily to show my ability, but to show how good Rohm Brothers calls were.

Even my daddy said, "All right, boy, this man done gave you some calls, you gotta sign up and call."

As a gift my daddy said he would even pay my entry fee for the contest, which at the time was about thirty-five dollars. He said, "You're gonna call. You ain't gonna chicken out. If you start something you're going to finish it. I don't care how bad you do, you're going to do your best."

So he signed me up. When I got there I was so nervous and felt totally outgunned. I remember seeing Ben Rogers Lee there, another turkey-calling icon; then I saw Chris and Dick Kirby and Joe Drake. All of these childhood icons of mine were walking around, belonging, fitting in, and I remember thinking, "What in the world am I doing here? I have gone and stepped right out of my ranks."

That's when I first realized how important it is to believe in yourself. I learned something else as well. Your friends, or, more accurately, those who you believe are your friends, don't always want to see you succeed. Ricky Joe, Mike, and Joe Drake all believed in me and bolstered my confidence, but many people who I thought were friends actually tried to bring me down, saying things like, "Dude, you are about to get embarrassed and get your ass whupped." It hurt my feelings, but it motivated me even more, if for no other reason than to prove them wrong. That is a funny thing about some people's nature. It is almost as if they know they wouldn't try if they were in your shoes, so they want to keep you from trying. I guess I just never understood that. I am sincerely as happy for a friend to do well as I am for myself to do well.

There were thirty-seven callers in the preliminary contest, and from them they picked the top twelve. I ended up placing fifth in that first round. After that I got some confidence and I actually beat some of the people that I thought were better callers than me. In the finals I ended up finishing fifth overall—I didn't win it, but I came away with some much-needed validation.

From that point on, my confidence was at an all-time high. I was part of the Rohm Brothers game-calling team (and had an official embroidered jacket to prove it) and as far as I was concerned was at the top of the world. Nothing else mattered. There was no money in it; in fact I was spending money just to compete, but I was around a group of people I liked. We talked about hunting, turkey calling, and all aspects of the outdoors.

It eventually turned out that Ricky Joe and myself started carpooling to contests. We were going everywhere to compete. And invariably, between myself, Joe Drake, and Ricky Joe, we would take the top three spots. Eventually I found myself at the Grand Nationals, competing against my boyhood idols like Paul Butski.

Calling competitions were just a fun pastime for me. I never saw them as a future or even a way to make money. It was just something I loved. By this point in my life, I was just out of high school and working for my dad while also going to heating and air-conditioning school. Heating and air-conditioning was my career plan. Hunting and calling were just passionate hobbies.

I thought I had my future all figured out. It just goes to show that one really never knows how life's cards will be dealt. Little did I know how calling competitions would change my career path—and ultimately my life.

Realtree Outdoors threw a big contest down in Perry, Georgia, called the Realtree Grand American. Up to that point I had won some small local contests, but I had never won a big one. The Realtree Grand American definitely counted as a "big one." The grand prize of $1,000 was sure tempting, but I was broker than a Chinaman working on a railroad and just couldn't swing the gas money and the entry fee, so I decided not to go. In the end, like so many times before, it was other people believing in me that literally changed my life. My father loaned me the money for gas to get down there and gave me the money for the entry fee, on the condition that I do my best and give him a quarter of the proceeds should I happen to win. Dad was always a shrewd businessman. He didn't know if I would win or not, but he figured it was a good enough gamble to risk the money.

Well, after yelping and clucking my way through the preliminaries into the main event, I ended up on the big stage and taking first place in the Grand American. It was just by happenstance that Bill Jordan, the head of Realtree, was in attendance. Dale Rohm was talking to him after the competition. I headed over there to thank Dale for believing in me all those years ago, giving me free game calls and encouraging me to compete. I had this big trophy in my hands and I was standing off to the side, waiting for him to finish talking, when Dale noticed me and said, "Well, speak of the devil. I was just telling Bill about you, saying what a good young man you are."

Bill looked at me, nodded his head, and said, "Dale's told me quite a bit about you. Have you ever thought about wearing some Realtree camouflage?"

I looked down at my Rohm Brothers jacket—which was Realtree—and said, "Mr. Jordan, I am already wearing it."

Bill smiled, realizing I wasn't catching his meaning. He said, "How about I give you a little better deal on that—how would you like to be on the Realtree advisory staff?"

I couldn't believe it. I was truly floored. Bill shook my hand and said, "It's a deal." From his pocket he took a business card, wrote down my sizes and address, and slipped it back in his pocket. That was all that was said.

Up until this point in my career, only Dale Rohm and my true friends had believed in me. And here Bill Jordan, the king of hunting in the South, was saying he wanted me to be part of his team. After we parted, however, I honestly didn't think anything would ever come of it.

It wasn't but three or four days later when Daddy and I came home from a job site and dang if there wasn't a huge box sitting by the door with Realtree printed on the side of it. Like kids at Christmas, Dad and I started tearing open the box. Inside there were three or four sets of Realtree clothing and an advisory staff contract.

Since I've had my role on the Outdoor Channel and some of the status that has come with it, people have asked me if I ever got bigheaded or too big for my britches. I hope anyone who knows me will tell ya that I am as down-to-earth today as I was before I ever got into the industry, but if there was ever a time when I may have gotten pretty proud of my accomplishments, it was right then and there for a brief period. At that moment I felt larger than life looking into that box of clothing. In my mind I had finally made the BIG TIME. There was nothing more I needed. I had free game calls and I had free camouflage and all I needed was a shotgun-shell sponsor and, son, in my mind I was Paul Butski. I was so pumped, me and my daddy were high-fiving and whooping it up. Daddy was going through the box, saying, "Well, these pants don't fit me, but this jacket does. I'll take the jacket if you want the pants . . ." We were snatching clothing back and forth, more like a couple of schoolgirls than a father and son.

As things would happen, within a few days I got another box and a letter, this time from Toxey Haas and Cuz Strickland at Mossy Oak. It was the nicest letter. It went on and on about how they had heard about me and wanted to let me know I was always welcome on the Mossy Oak hunting team, and in that box was a bunch of Mossy Oak camouflage. Up until this point of my life I had worn Realtree and Mossy Oak, and now I had free sets of both.

And now I was torn. To be honest, I was a fan of both camouflage companies. And I was extremely flattered that either of these companies believed enough in me to send me clothes and want me to be associated with them. So I talked to my dad and asked him what he thought I should do.

Like always, he gave first-rate advice. "Well, you need to make a decision. You owe one of them a conversation and one of them a commitment."

So even though I didn't know him from Adam, I called Cuz Strickland and had a long conversation with him. He was extremely nice and supportive of me. I said, "Cuz, I am a big fan of what you all do, but I am from Georgia. Realtree is a Georgia company and Bill Jordan shook my hand and said he believed in me and sent me a box of clothes, and I feel like I owe it to Mr. Jordan to wear his clothes. But you don't know how much it means to me to know you guys believe in me as well, and I will always be honored that you sent me that box. If you like I can send these clothes back."

"No, Michael, wear 'em if you can, wear 'em if you want to or give 'em away. We are just glad you called."

Even though I eventually worked for their competitors for over a decade, I never had any ill feelings toward anyone at Mossy Oak. Because of the way they treated me, I have always considered them a class act.

I kept calling in competitions and did well over the years. Oh, I never turned into a "great" like Paul Butski or Dick Kirby, but calling taught me a lot about the outdoors and made me a lot of great friends that I still have to this day. And I learned a thing or two about turkey hunting along the way.

5

YOUR HUNTING BUDDIES
ARE EVERYTHING

After graduating high school, I was still living at home. I had finished heating and air-conditioning school but still helped out my father's contracting business. One of my duties was to check the answering machine when I got home from work. One day I came home and played the messages and there was one from David Blanton of Realtree, whom I had briefly gotten to know through my advisory staff position.

"Hey, buddy, this is David Blanton. I was just gonna holler at ya and see if you would be available to help us guide some turkey hunters. I don't know what your schedule looks like, but we got a bunch of outdoor writers coming down and we could use some help guiding them."

As soon as I heard this, I thought, "I'm in!" I didn't need an excuse to turkey hunt, and to do it with the

Realtree guys and some outdoor writers was icing on the cake. In my mind I had already said yes, but then, just before hanging up, David added:

"Oh, and by the way, we will pay you a hundred dollars a day for guiding."

My jaw simply hit the floor. It was too good to be true. I would have gone hunting for nothin', and now they were going to pay me!

When my dad got home I told him about it and asked him if I could get the time off to spend a week guiding them. He said, "Well, that sounds like a pretty good deal. Why don't you give it a shot? Who knows what will happen, but it may turn out to be a pretty good opportunity for ya."

Some people think of hunters as solitary types, and we do spend time alone in the woods, trying to go one-on-one with game. But like I learned from my daddy, the relationships you make hunting, whether with family, friends, or strangers, are as important as the kills you make. When the date arrived, I drove down to camp. I remember pulling up and feeling so intimidated and out of my league. There was Joe Drake, Terry Rohm, Betty Lou and Tom Fegley, Kathy Etling, and a couple of outdoor writers I didn't know. One in particular was Laura Lee Dovey. When I pulled up she was gallivanting around camp, kinda boisterous and having fun. She reminded me of a cheerleader, and I remember thinking, "I hope I can guide her, she seems like she would be easy to get along with."

She must have felt the same about me, because as soon as my truck came to a stop, she ran over and introduced herself and immediately told Bill Jordan, "I want to go hunting with this young man." Well, if you know Laura, if she says it's so, it's set in stone. Bill wasn't going to argue with her, so I was her guide.

The next morning, I took Laura over to some property that Bill sent me to that he had leased for this hunt. We tried and tried but could not even strike a bird on the roost, let alone call one in. I don't know if Bill sent me on a wild-goose chase or what, but we couldn't locate a turkey anywhere all of that day or the next. But while we were getting skunked, Laura and I were having a blast nonetheless. We were cutting up and enjoying the hunt, and I realized early on, while killing a turkey is always nice, having a good time is really important.

Well, by the end of the second day I was starting to get a mite worried. I had gotten good at turkey calling, but turkey killin' was a different story. And the fact that the other guides in camp were turkey assassins only made it worse. Not to mention, I was surrounded by a bunch of outdoor writers who were also hunting professionals and celebrities. I thought I needed to impress Laura. So I called my good friend and brother-in-law, the owner of the Hunting Shack, Shane Collier. Shane was one of the best hunters I have ever known in Meriwether County. He always killed nice deer with his bow, and he was killing turkeys around Manchester before anybody was. If anyone could help me out it would be Shane.

So I called him and said, "Shane, I need some help. I got this outdoor writer woman with me and I can't even buy a turkey at the Piggly Wiggly. I have taken her everywhere Bill has said and it's just not working out. We haven't heard so much as a gobble!"

"Bring her back home, Michael. You know the country here, and I got several other great spots with some hot birds. Surely we can get her on a bird around your place."

So I took his advice and brought Laura back to Booger Bottom to hunt the family place, as well as some ground Shane and I knew. Before I knew it she was eatin' dinner with me and my dad, hangin' out with the family, and having a grand ole time. We hunted for another day or so. In the end we didn't get a turkey, but we did start a lifelong friendship.

Even though I couldn't manage to call in a turkey, Laura saw something in me. Laura thought that I had something different. She went back to Bill and said, "Bill, I just met a future superstar in the hunting industry." When she told me that, I knew she was exaggerating but I was sure flattered.

Laura took me under her wing and was committed to helping me get involved in the outdoor industry. She would call me constantly and instructed me to write letters to Bill Jordan and David Blanton and thank them for the guiding opportunity they gave me.

Well, I got through that spring and summer (with Laura's coaching) and lo and behold if Steve Lamboy, the VP of licensing at Realtree, didn't call me!

"Hey, Michael, I might need you to help me work a few shows this year. Matter of fact, I need you to work the Buckmaster Jam, which is coming up soon in Atlanta. Can you make it?"

"Yeah, I guess so . . ." I said hesitantly.

"Great, I need you there next weekend. You'll find a lady named Ashley Snipes and a DJ Watkins—they'll meet you there and instruct you on what to do." With that he hung up.

So I drove up to Atlanta in my little ole jacked-up, muddy Toyota pickup truck. I was so nervous, as I had never driven in a big city, but I finally made it to the Georgia Dome, where the show was being held.

I got to the Realtree booth before the show started. I was walking around and sure enough I found these two young girls, Ashley and DJ. At the time they were in charge of sales at Realtree. I was wearing some Levi's jeans that were a little too long so I had them turned under with a pair of boots.

I walked up and said, "Are you Ashley?"

She said, "Yeah, I am Ashley, and you must be Michael."

"That's right. Steve wasn't real clear on exactly what I was to do, but he said you would tell me."

She took a stern look down her nose at me and said in all seriousness, "Well, first thing you need to do is fix your pants—that ain't the style. You don't roll blue jeans under, you need to roll them up."

Those were the first words Ashley ever said to me. I was utterly intimidated by her frankness, and I immediately did as I was told. It is a tradition I carry on to this day. You see, several years later Ashley became my wife.

While I was bent over, following her jean-rolling instructions, DJ walked up, smiled, and said, "Hey, I'm DJ," and stuck out her hand. "Okay," I thought, "the less bossy of the two."

Before I could finish my assessment of her, she continued with: "Go get some of those boxes and start unpacking them."

In other words, in a matter of less than five minutes of meeting these two girls, they had let me know they were in charge, put me in my place, and put me straight to work.

While we were unpacking the boxes, Ashley said, "So I hear you're a good turkey caller . . . *or whatever*, but what we need you to do here is help sell Team Realtree hats, shirts, and videos."

At the end of that first day, myself, Ashley, DJ, and several other people working the show all went to dinner at some fancy Italian restaurant. Now, keep in mind, I didn't grow up poor, but I grew up simple. I had never been to a super-duper fancy restaurant. The fanciest I had been to was Shogun, the Japanese steakhouse where they cook in front of ya, throwing those knives up and tossing eggs in their hats and stuff like that. It seemed like every girl I dated in high school, that was their favorite place to eat in Columbus, Georgia.

Now here I am in the big metropolis of Atlanta, around traffic, crowds, and cultures I had never experienced, and here we are at this fancy restaurant and they are ordering all these appetizers. I am thinking, "Good night, they're gonna have forty dollars of appetizers before we even eat!" I am looking at the menu and it's all this Italian stuff I don't even know how to pronounce. The lowest-priced item I can find is a twenty-four-dollar meal. I am asking myself, "Do I really just order this?" There is no way I am spending twenty-four dollars on some fancy spaghetti, so I nudge Ashley and ask, "Who's buying this?"

"Oh, order what you want, this is compliments of Bill Jordan and Realtree."

The only thing that sounded right was lasagna . . . it was a twenty-four-dollar lasagna dish which turned out didn't taste no better than what my momma used to make.

When the bill came it was like three hundred and seventy-something dollars, and I remember thinking, "You know what? I have went to Hollywood! This is big time, and all I done was help sell some videos and hats."

The whole corporate culture was plain shocking to me, as I grew up working construction with my dad, which was totally different. When his employees went to work, at lunchtime they either had five dollars to buy McDonald's or they didn't eat. It wasn't my dad's responsibility to feed them. I grew up in a culture where if you were out there working on a job and you hurt yourself—guess what? You're hurt, and you're not working, and you ain't gonna get paid.

So this world was completely foreign to me. All I was doing was helping Bill out by selling some videos and he was putting me up, buying my meals, and not only that, he was paying me a hundred dollars a day to boot! I had a hard time fathoming that. It really made me appreciate working for Realtree. No matter what we were doing, I always tried to give more, and always tried to be the first one there and the last one to leave, because I truly appreciated the job.

During that show I did my best for Mr. Jordan. The way I figured it, this man had given me a chance and was paying me to work for him, so I needed to give him my all. I was constantly restacking the videos so they looked nice, reorganizing all the other merchandise, and greeting every customer with a smile. I tried to present Realtree in the very best light.

I am not a city person, but working that sports show was one of the best times I ever had. I was around good folks, I was meeting people in the outdoor industry and eating fancy food that I couldn't pronounce. If I hadn't had such a good time guidin' Laura Lee Dovey, without a single turkey to show for it, I would never have been there.

6

CAMERA HUNTIN'

It is harder to hunt with a bow than with a rifle. I was about to learn that it's even harder to hunt with a camera. Over the course of that next year, I worked some more consumer shows for Realtree and did some more competition calling, and before I knew it, the following year had rolled around and like clockwork I got another call from David Blanton.

"Hey, Michael, not only do we want you to guide this year, but we are interested in you helping run a camera for our video department."

The previous spring, when guiding, I showed David some of the footage me and Shane Collier had taken of killing some turkeys and some good Georgia whitetails with both bows and rifles.

I said, "David, really? I don't know if I can run those cameras y'all got. You got them big, fancy cameras I ain't never worked with. All I have ever done is video on simple VHS stuff, not those Betacams you all have."

David said, "Look, if you're a cameraman you're a cameraman. You don't necessarily have to have schooling or have an inside knowledge about a camera. You either have an eye for photography or you don't. I think you have a good eye for video work, and I think you could run our cameras. Why don't you come down here and we'll give you some basic instruction."

So, in early February I drove down to Realtree's headquarters and met with David and was introduced to his right-hand man, Steve Finch. At the time, the two of them comprised all of Realtree's video department.

Steve was a kid from California who grew up dreaming of producing TV and movies. His life was all about video production. David sent me upstairs and told me to sit down with Steve for a while and go over their Betacams. In a nutshell, Steve was going to give me a very basic, redneck primer on how to run them. It was apparent during our first meeting that Steve was very intellectual and very wordy in the way he described things.

Well, Steve was talking to me, describing these cameras, and talking in a language I didn't begin to understand. Steve's world was a world of white balances, shutter speeds, irises, and apertures—all stuff that went so far over my head that I was as lost as a duck decoy without a string. But I pretended to act like I knew what he was talking about, nodding my head at what I thought was the appropriate time and injecting the occasional "uh-huh"—like I was an old hand with irises and such. I was thinking the whole time, "If I can just get this camera in my hands, figure out where the on-and-off switch is, with some time and a couple of tapes I can screw up enough to where I'll eventually get it right."

After the brief instructional lecture, I walked back downstairs to meet with David. Steve walked down with me. David said, "Steve, why don't you go back upstairs and get a package ready, one of those new Betacams. I want to send it home with Michael." Now here was David Blanton telling Steve to go get a sixty-thousand-dollar camera to send off to Booger Bottom, Georgia, with a redneck turkey hunter. I immediately got nervous—I mean, this camera package was worth more than me and my daddy's house.

"I know you'll figure it out," David continued. "You have a good eye for it. In two weeks I want you to go to Florida to film an Osceola turkey hunt with me, Bill Jordan, Steve Finch, Brad Harris, and Ricky Joe Bishop."

My first thought was how in the world am I gonna get to Florida. That is an expensive and long ride to get south of Tampa to hunt Osceolas. Once again my nonunderstanding of corporate culture was coming through.

Hesitantly I replied, "Wow . . . that's great, but how long of a drive is that?"

"No, no, no, buddy. We're gonna fly."

Well, I had never flown anywhere before, so immediately I got even more nervous.

Keep in mind, I hadn't even turned one of those newfangled, highfalutin Betacams on yet! I didn't know even how to run it, and here David Blanton is telling me I am going to do just fine. I am glad he believed in my ability, since I sure as heck didn't.

Once again, I found that every time people believed in me, from my dad, to Dale, to Bill Jordan to Laura Lee Dovey to now David, I always had a better chance of delivering because I felt that I couldn't let them down.

I left Realtree with a plane ticket to Tampa, a sixty-thousand-dollar Betacam, and a pickup-load of no experience on how to run it. All I knew was how to turkey-call, how to bowhunt, how to field dress stuff, and how to build corners and T's for my dad's construction business. And here I was, getting the opportunity to run a camera for Realtree Outdoors and go hunting with David Blanton and Bill Jordan. So I went straight home, figured out how to turn the camera on, and got the basics down filming around the house. It is easy to video trees, clouds, leaves, and cars going down the road. It is completely different to film wildlife.

It was the middle of February, and in the South the birds will start gobbling early, so I had a bunch of buddies who were already out scouting them. Heck, some of those old boys probably even had some long-beards in the freezer, even though the season didn't come in until the third week of March.

So I called Ricky Joe and said, "Hey, brother, looks like I am going to Florida with y'all to run a camera. I don't know if I will be filming you or who, but I got a brand-new Realtree camera over here and I don't even know how to run it. We ought to get up in the morning and go see if we can't hear a turkey gobble and call him in so I can videotape it."

He agreed and we made plans for the following morning.

The following morning at five thirty we were perched on a little old overlook where we knew a bunch of turkeys were roosted over in FDR State Park. All we had were some turkey calls, some Realtree clothing, and a brand-new camera. Ricky was gonna try and work some into range and I was going to see if I could video them.

So it was the crack of dawn and I was going through all the settings, trying to figure out how to white-balance, figuring out what the gain was and what filter to shoot it on, and sure enough we got a turkey to gobble, then a couple more. In no time we could hear them coming. Within minutes of first hearing them, here comes a gobbler in full strut. He came up through there gobbling his head off, and before I know it I had videoed this joker for thirty to forty minutes before he finally walked off.

Ricky Joe whispered, "Well, did you get it?"

"Yeah, I'm pretty sure I got it. I don't know if I got it with the right filter or white balance, but I tried to remember everything Steve told me to do. I think I shot it right."

So I immediately got on the phone, and by this time it's maybe seven thirty, and called David Blanton.

After a couple of rings he picked up.

"Who's this?"

"This is Michael."

"Well, what are ya doin', man? How's that camera?"

"It's fine. I am on my way to Columbus right now. What time you get to work? I want to show you some of this footage I shot this morning."

With a chuckle David replied, "What did you shoot this morning, some cars, clouds, and leaves around the house?"

"Naw, I did that yesterday. This morning I got a turkey strutting around and gobbling and doing everything you wanted him to do."

David went silent for a bit, and then said, "You got a turkey strutting and gobbling? You filmed turkeys this morning? I just gave you that camera yesterday."

"Well, that's what I thought you wanted me to learn to do."

"That is awesome! Man, if you want to drive back down here to Columbus, come on. I'd love to see that footage."

So I burned it up to Columbus, popped that Beta tape in, and hit play. We all sat around, watching this gobbler perform on cue. When he was finished, David said, "Mike, that is awesome footage. I can't believe you got that this morning."

But one thing about David is, he always shoots ya straight. "The white balance is dead on," he continued, "but you shot the footage a little dark."

Steve was there, too, as was Bill Jordan, and they were kinda laughin' because they knew they were dealing with a straight-up country-boy redneck. Here it was middle of February . . . how was I supposed to know the turkeys would be gobbling? Obviously, I had been out there before. You could tell they wanted to ask, "So, have you killed a turkey yet this spring?" But they never did.

I went to Florida nervous as a freakin' cat, and got even more nervous when David told me that I would be filming Bill Jordan. I remember thinking, "Why in the world is David sending me with Bill? Bill is the big dog of this company, and I am the greenest rookie."

In retrospect, if you got right down to it, the truth of the matter was that Ricky Joe and Brad Harris were better turkey hunters than Bill, and so David and Steve went with the best odds of killing a turkey (which proved to be true). By the second day, both of them had turkeys stacked up, while Bill and I were still out there, trying to bowhunt a turkey. We couldn't kill nothin'.

I was getting frustrated, thinking, "Dang . . . Bill is not as good a turkey hunter as I thought he would have been." From the outside looking in, I'd figured Bill was surrounded by game every time he went out, which I learned was not the case. But while he may not have been a downright turkey assassin, the biggest thing that impressed me about Bill was what kind of person he was. He is a lot of fun to be around. We were laughing and cutting up when the first turkey gobbled. When I realized that bird was committed and coming in, I got so nervous. The realization that I, a young country kid, was filming for a major network, for a major production company, with their main man, it all hit me like a ton of bricks.

I was scared to death that I was going to screw it up. As it turned out, two jakes came strutting in there and Bill let them walk. Bill and I ended up staying a couple extra days and finally Bill killed a turkey with his bow. This kicked off a whole spring of work for me. I ended up filming Bill kill an entire Slam with his bow. I went on every trip Realtree made that spring, earning a hundred dollars a day as a freelance camera guy, and when I wasn't running a camera, I was guiding for them.

As a gift for working hard, when we went to Texas, Bill offered to let me kill a turkey on film. However, the full deal was I had to kill one with my bow first. If I could kill one with my bow, then I could kill one with my shotgun, on camera. But Bill didn't put any stipulations on what size turkey I had to kill with my bow. So the next morning when the first big ole jake came strutting in, I waxed him just so I could get to my shotgun. We went out the next day and I shot a good long-beard with my shotgun as well. That was the first time I was ever on video—it turned up on the *All-Stars of Spring* video that year.

The spring turkey season finally came to an end in May and I had videoed the Realtree guys all the way to the end. By spending time with David I realized how busy a person he was and how much responsibility he had. I was always so eager to be around the Realtree crowd, I was like a kid in a candy store. I was always asking them questions and talking their ears off. I felt more like a fan than a member of the staff. So when the season came to an end, I felt like I had taken too much of their time, and I thought, "Well, I am going to give it a little while, I don't want to wear these guys out, pestering them to death and overstaying my welcome." I was about to relearn a lesson Laura Lee Dovey had taught me: you gotta stay in touch.

I went back to work for my dad in construction and was thinking about getting back into the heating and cooling industry and just generally trying to figure out what direction my life was going to take. Then about two weeks later, I got a message on the answering machine from David and from the sound in his voice, he sounded a little bit upset with me. The message went something like this:

"Michael, this is David. I am a little bit disappointed. I don't know what we did to make you mad or piss you off, but I would appreciate a phone call."

I was shocked. I wasn't mad or pissed, I was just trying to be respectful and stay out of their hair. Here I was, this young kid from Booger Bottom who was just very thankful for the opportunity I had to help Realtree and make some money that spring, and I didn't want to seem like a pest.

So I called David and tentatively said "Hey, David, Michael here. Is everything cool?"

"Yeah, everything is cool. Everything cool with you?"

"Yeah, I'm fine."

"Well, I was just wondering . . . I thought we had a great spring, and here it's been three weeks and you ain't even called back and said nothing."

"Well, David, to be honest with ya, I felt like I done bugged y'all to death and I kinda wanted to give you a chance to catch your breath. I know how busy you are, as I heard your phone ringing off the hook this spring, with people pulling at you and Bill and different companies calling, not to mention the writers and manufacturers always pulling at ya. No, I ain't mad, in fact I was praying you would call me. But I didn't know you was going to be mad when you finally did."

"Well, then get your butt back up here, I got a proposal for ya."

So I drove back up to Columbus and met with David Blanton and he made me an offer to work for Realtree's production department full-time. This was a dream come true. All spring I had thought about the possibility of getting a chance to do exactly that for a living, and every night when I went to bed I prayed that would be in my future.

My grandmomma used to say that if you get a chance to do what you love for a living, it's worth more than any amount of money in the world. I hoped she was right, because David offered me $18,000 a year. As much as I loved the job, I knew it was going to be hard to pay the bills on that kind of salary, but I took the job anyway. And you know what? My grandmomma was always right.

My job was not to be an on-camera personality, but to be a cameraman, to help guide writers and learn to edit and potentially produce turkey and deer videos. To be honest, I didn't ever think what $18,000 panned out to be per hour. Come to find out, with all the hours I put in at Realtree, including all the time on the road, it probably averaged out to about fifty cents an hour. But I loved doing what I was doing so much I never thought or cared about how much time I was putting into it or how much money I was making.

I learned a lot. I got the chance to be around people who really knew the business, and eventually I got the opportunity to edit shows, and got to know some of the folks at TNN. As my video-editing knowledge grew, I got more comfortable with the process and in turn started coming up with some new ideas on how to edit a show. That was one of the cool things about Bill and David—they were never threatened by new ideas or new ways of looking at things. They gave me a lot of rope to try out new ideas.

As I got more involved with Realtree and became a regular contributor to their production department, David decided to send me to a videography school in Maine. It was a great school, but to this day I have never met more liberal, left-wing goofballs in my life who totally didn't understand me, my friends, or my culture. Ninety percent of the people up there looked at me like I was the Antichrist because I took pride in killing animals. I realized that not everybody was from Booger Bottom and enjoyed going out and double-lunging a deer with a bow, taking it home, and marinating backstraps to feed the family. I realized there were vegetarians and vegans out there, even people who didn't wear leather shoes or belts! To me, these were really freaky, scary people that I was nervous to be around.

But I had to stick it out in this liberal world, even though I was as country as corn bread and about as out of place as a turd in a punch bowl. The way I figured it, my goal was to learn how to edit so I could get back home and make Realtree happy with my production abilities. If I had to tolerate some nut jobs for a while, so be it.

David had given me unrestricted access to the Realtree library of raw footage, which was a dream come true for any hunter. I had all this footage of nearly everybody in the world—my world, that is—from Jim Zumbo to Bill Jordan to David Blanton to Dale Earnhardt, Sr.—all with kill shots. I selected the best of the best tapes and brought them up to Maine with me. To my way of thinking, I had everything I needed to make a masterpiece. I was so excited just to have it, I figured some of my fellow students would be just as excited—I knew my buddies like Shane Collier and Ricky Joe back home would love to see it. However, when I showed it to my fellow classmates, they looked at me like I was Satan.

Right away several people in the class protested and said they wouldn't have any part of celebrating the killing of animals. So get this: I had to sit down with a couple of people they put on my "team" and edit only the hunts where the deer got away. That was the compromise the school worked out. This made me some kind of mad.

At the end of the course, on the last night they had a nice dinner and we had to show our productions to the whole school. The school had some Rolling Rock beer on tap during this final night production showing.

Now, I have never been a big drinker, but I do like a cold one from time to time. But feeling depressed and aggravated on account of these liberal numb nuts, I was ready to tip at least one cold one back. The more I drank, the more I thought about the fact that I was surrounded by people who were completely foreign to my way of life and thinking. These people didn't hunt, fish, or love the outdoors. They had never killed a rabbit and made biscuits and gravy with it. Hell, these people didn't even know who Lynyrd Skynyrd or Hank Williams, Jr., were. If I was a culture shock for them, they were an earthquake for me. Sitting there, contemplating this, I done had me two or three big ole glasses of that Rollin' Rock to calm my nerves.

In the middle of dinner the instructor stood up and said, "The next project you are going to see, of which we are very proud, is entitled *The Deer Getaway Production*, produced and directed by Michael Waddell and his team. Michael, would you care to say a few words?"

This was totally unexpected; I was not prepared to say anything about the project.

I had never done any public speaking, but I walked up there on stage and got the microphone and said, "Well, obviously y'all know I ain't from around here by the way I talk . . . and neither do I really want to be from around here. I am a hunter and I am proud to be a hunter...I work for a company called Realtree Outdoors. Our show can be seen on TNN. The Nashville Network for those of you who may not know. We celebrate the outdoors, and we don't mind laying the smackdown on big deer and turkeys. The following presentation is one my group created, but I am totally against it because all of these deer you are about to see are edited to get away. Just so you know, every one of them is dead and has been eaten by now. Thank you . . . I'm Michael Waddell." And I proceeded back to the Rolling Rock keg and tapped me another big glass of beer.

There was no applause.

This was the first time I felt like my culture was being judged, and I didn't like it. These people were looking down at me, the way I was raised, my family, my friends, and what I stood for. It was an eye-opener.

I returned to Realtree a little older and a little wiser to the ways of the world.

To the school's credit, I learned a lot about editing and the time spent there made me a much better producer than I was before. And while it made me pretty darn uncomfortable to spend so much time among antihunting liberals, it only made me that much more committed to promoting my own culture and lifestyle.

7

WHAT YOU SEE MAY NOT BE WHAT YOU GET

Before I went to work for Realtree I was just like everyone else who watched their *Monster Bucks* videos. I just assumed if you went to some of the places you saw in the shows that your hunt would be an immediate success. I figured if you went to the hot spots, like Kansas, Illinois, or Canada, you were almost guaranteed a 160- or 170-inch buck. I used to think Bill Jordan must be a pretty good deer hunter, but he ain't killed one in Booger Bottom! If I could go to some of those places, I am sure I could kill an ole monster just like Bill.

But after I started working full-time for Realtree I found out a whitetail deer is a whitetail deer, no matter where it lives. The only thing that changes is the potential for big deer—and there is never a guarantee. There is no place (where it is fair chase) where easy Boone and Crockett deer are just hiding behind every bush. I have had hard hunting for whitetails all over the country. I learned that lesson on one of my first big trips filming for Realtree in Saskatchewan, Canada.

It's obvious to anyone who ever hears me talk that I am no northern boy. I got lots of southern blood in me. When I got to Saskatoon, Saskatchewan, it was one of the coldest years they ever had on record. I got off the plane and I remember walking down the breezeway, thinking, "Man! The heat in the airport must not be on." I had my jacket on and I was still cold. Oh, the heat was on, it was just so cold outside they couldn't keep the place a comfortable temperature. Well, we got out of the terminal and were waiting for outfitter Brian Hoffman to pick us up at the curb when I realized how truly cold it was. I took one breath and the inside of my nose froze solid. I was not experienced with much outside my home area, so I didn't know how to deal with this, and it started to freak me out. I was thinking, "Am I the only one whose nose is freezing?" So I started trying to breath through my mouth, looking sidelong at everyone else to see if they were panicking about their noses freezing. Within thirty seconds of standing outside, on the curb, my nose was frozen as solid as a Minnesota farm pond. When Brian arrived, we all jumped into the truck. He had the radio going, and to this day I will never forget the warning I heard come across the airwaves. I had never heard such a message before, nor do I hope to ever hear it again as long as I live. It was "the eyeball warning." The temperature outside was something like 25 to 30 below zero, and they were advising people to blink every so many seconds so that their eyeballs didn't freeze! Now, of course, what that meant to me was that we were absolute morons if we thought we were going deer hunting in this weather. How in the world were we going to hunt when all we could think about was our eyeballs freezing solid?

But we had traveled a long way from Georgia to get there and we were going to hunt, even though the mercury had dropped south of the Mason-Dixon line. Now, when hunting in Canada, they put you out on stand an hour before daybreak and they pick you up an hour after dark. We had several hunters and cameramen in camp. My role was to film Bill Jordan, and even though I had filmed Bill before, I was still a rookie, so doing the job right was a big deal. I wanted to make sure I did my best. The first morning we get up in our stand and there ain't even a seat, just bare metal. There is nothing quite as miserable as spending a full day with a numb backside frozen to a metal seat. Even though I had on every layer of clothes that I owned, I still nearly froze to death! In a full day of sitting, we only saw two deer. I realized right there that Canada wasn't going to be as fun or as easy as I had anticipated.

Bill had decided to make the "wise" choice of bow-hunting, which I later realized was about as jacked up as a snake in a weed eater. Because not only was it so cold and still that the noise carried horribly far, but later, when he did try to draw, he was so cold and had so many clothes on he couldn't get the bow back. While I love bowhunting, there are times when the odds are so stacked against ya by Mother Nature that you should do yourself a favor and use a rifle.

Well, it quickly became obvious that in this super-cold weather there were no deer moving, and about the only thing I could look forward to on this hunt was lunchtime. There was a little Indian girl cook in the camp who would make us sandwiches and put together a lunch sack for us, but by noon that lunch was frozen harder than five dollars' worth of jawbreakers. I realized, however, that I could stuff chemical hand warmers inside my muff and put this great carrot cake she made inside with it. By lunchtime it would be so nice and warm and toasty the frosting would almost be melting off of it.

Bill had observed me doing this, but Bill is so incredibly anal about movement or noise in the stand that he wouldn't think of doing the same with his carrot cake. Even to this day I honestly believe that Bill will tell ya that he has never spooked a deer in the stand—it was always someone else. So . . . anytime he heard any kind of rustle (even if he made it), he looked toward the cameraman—which in this case was me.

We hadn't seen a deer in what seemed like seventeen days. In reality it had been four or five. So I was doing everything I could to postpone eating my carrot cake, 'cause that was the high point of the day, with no deer around. The way I figured it, the more hours I burned up before this great event, the less time I would have to kill afterward with nothing to look forward to. It finally got to about noon and I reached into the muff and got this steaming piece of carrot cake out. I had it in one hand, trying to unwrap it as quietly and stealthily as I could so as not to disturb Bill, when suddenly he looked up and started freaking out, whispering, "Big buck! Big buck!" The first thing I did is fire up the camera, but I was aware enough not to drop the carrot cake. So I've got the carrot cake in one hand and the camera in the other when I start looking for this deer. While I'm searching through the flurries of snow, I feel something bump my cake hand. I look over at Bill and it's pretty easy to see what's happened. Now, Bill Jordan has a pretty big smeller on him, and there was vanilla icing all over it. I looked down in fear at my hand holding the cake. In one bite, Bill had pretty much destroyed my carrot cake! As it turned out, of course, there was no "big buck."

He thought it was the funniest thing in the world. To me it was a matter of life and death. At that point, had I had a weapon, I would have killed him right there.

Eventually I got over the carrot cake incident, but I'll tell ya, hunting in Canada isn't for everyone. The deer were few and far between, and there was a whole mess of between. We sat there from morning until night without leaving the stand. To kill the time I reflected on my childhood, and my life up to that point, which since I was only twenty-one years old wasn't that much. Finally, I turned to Bill and said:

"Bill, it occurs to me now that I am way too young to be hunting Canada. Because, sitting here, I have already thought about every last thing I have done in my life at least three times, and right now I have zero to think about that entertains me, so if you could just tell me some of the things you have done, 'cause you're a lot older than me, I could just sit here and think about those things for a while. I have already thought about all my loves, every baseball I ever hit, every home run I ever got, every girl I dated, every girl I should have dated, every turkey-calling contest I was in, every turkey I killed, every deer I killed, every football game I played in, and I have absolutely totally nothing left to think about. I'm miserable, and if this pull-up rope is strong enough, I might tie it around my neck and jump out now."

Bill just looked at me, shook his head, smiled slightly, and looked back out into the flurries of blowing snow, never saying a word.

Well, after I hit that all-time low in the field, this hunt went on for another thirteen or so days. On day eighteen of the hunt Bill finally pulled the trigger on about a 145-inch buck. That was the Realtree reality— what happened in the field was not always as exciting as it appeared on TV. This hunt was one of my first major editing projects, and when you watch that episode, you probably think that there was a deer under every other tree up there in Saskatchewan. But in reality we spent eighteen days of videoing, with three cameras and three good hunters, to capture one 145-inch deer. This trip made me realize the price that had to be paid for good video production. Videoing hunts is not always a piece of cake: it takes a lot of hard work, perseverance, and a bit of luck to make it all come together.

My chance to be in front of the camera came thanks to a combination of several things. I wasn't making a lot of money working as a cameraman. But it was, and still is, part of the Realtree culture that the camera guys got to do a bit of hunting, as a perk or a thank-you. Basically, as a thank-you, Realtree would reward me with the biggest cookie they could—the chance to hunt. Now, anything that Realtree did, no matter who was hunting, we videoed. It was that simple. We were into television production and always looking for entertaining hunts. And you never know when the monster is going to hit the ground, so we filmed everything.

As I said, I was a cameraman then, but because of my turkey-calling background and the way I got involved with Realtree in the first place as a guide, I was also kinda considered an advisory or pro staff member as well. So I was something of a spokesperson for turkey tips on our *Memories of Spring* videos, and at least once or twice a year I was getting a chance to kill a turkey or two on camera.

My first opportunity to hunt deer on camera came about partly as a thank-you and partly thanks to David's belief in my skills as an archer. I had worked at the Big Buck Trading Post, so I knew how to set up a bow and knew quite a bit about archery and could work on equipment. David had seen me shoot around camp, so he had some confidence in my bowhunting ability. The first bowhunt I got to do on film was for a buck on the Encinitas Ranch in Texas. It was January and the SHOT show was going on, so while Bill, David, and the rest of the folks were going to SHOT, I got a chance to go on down to the Encinitas Ranch. We had one of the toughest years ever filming *Monster Bucks IV*, and they needed some more bowhunts, so I got the nod to go. Since the other cameramen were either busy or at the trade show, I brought my brother-in-law, Shane Collier, with me to run the camera. Bill had a stand on an oat field, and there were several nice bucks coming in there. We hunted for four or five days for them and just had a blast. I was shooting javelinas and hogs and just having a good time, but I wasn't having any luck on the big boys we knew were in the area. The Encinitas is a 40,000-acre ranch, and they had no other clients at the time. We had the place to ourselves, so we spent a lot of time just exploring. Shane and I were hunting out of a couple of tripod stands over this lush green oat field, and the first night this nine-pointer comes out and he is a pretty daggum good one, about 135 inches.

So this buck walks right up there and gets to about 30 yards and turns broadside. So I pulled back and just put the ole green weeny on him. I am here to tell you—I just smoked him. He ran just a little ways and fell dead. I was excited, and Shane is jumping around, high-fiving. So I get back to camp and call David who was at dinner with Bill and some other folks at the SHOT show.

"David, I just killed a good deer and got it on video."

"Man, that is awesome, Michael. I am fired up for ya!"

He then put Bill on the phone and Bill said, "Did you get you a good deer?"

"Yes sir," I replied. "He ain't a huge buck, but he is a good deer and we got him on camera."

"Well, there are a lot of deer down there, go kill another one," he replied.

When he said that, I couldn't believe it. I was some kind of pumped. I went out the next afternoon and hammered another big nine-pointer. I immediately got on the phone with Bill, and when I told him the news, he said, "That's great, Michael. Now get on a plane and come home, you're done."

"You mad at me, Bill?"

"Naw, I ain't mad at ya, but two's enough. See ya when ya get home."

By now I was really confident in my ability. I always knew I could kill deer by myself, but now I knew I could do it with the camera rolling. So I started thinking that maybe I was ready to call myself a professional. Yeah, that was a pretty impressive-sounding label.

. . .

My first appearance in a hunting video was in *Monster Bucks IV.* To be honest, I just couldn't believe it: *Monster Bucks* was the mac daddy of videos, and I was going to be in it. I was shocked as well as flattered. It was quite an honor.

Now that I was becoming a regular on the videos and TV, and had completed my producer school, I was given the title of producer and I started working more closely with David and Bill on the direction of Realtree Productions. I was now going to the TNN production meetings up at Nashville and taking a more active role in the operation.

The longer I was with Realtree, the more my roles got split between running a camera and producing, on the one hand, and being on camera, on the other. As time progressed, almost half of the time I was in front of the camera and the other half behind it.

I really enjoyed this. I was now getting a say, maybe only a small one, but a say nonetheless as to what I found entertaining. Ever since I realized that there were people out there who didn't like my lifestyle and culture, I was committed to promoting it to the best of my ability, but at the same time making it entertaining. Realtree Productions gave me the platform to do both.

The following year, Bill once again gave me an opportunity to go back to the Encinitas to hunt again. This time I was a tad more cocky than the previous year. I was sitting in a stand on a different part of the ranch when I looked up and saw this monster working his way toward me. This was a nice buck—a solid 145- to 150-class eight-pointer. As he was coming, I was already thinking this deer is just a few minutes away from riding in the back of my truck. The trail he was on would lead him right by my stand. So as he closed the gap to 10 yards I came to full draw and waited. All of a sudden the wind shifted and the deer stopped like he caught a bit of our scent. He was at 6 yards. I put my 20-yard pin right at the bottom of the hairline, thinking the arrow will hit a couple of inches high at that distance, blowing a hole right through his heart. This was obviously a mistake on my part as when a deer is that close the arrow will hit considerably lower. The arrow hit right at the bottom of the brisket, just cutting hair.

I had missed! It was and still is the most humbling miss of my life. I have never been so crushed. I couldn't sleep for the next two or three nights. I was so mad at myself for blowing such a good opportunity on such a good deer. That being said, it was probably a good thing. It brought me down a notch, as after that first year I had been something of a cocky kid, running around camp wondering how "professionals" could miss deer at close ranges and telling anyone who would listen that I would never do such a thing. It just goes to show, it can happen to anyone, at any time, and it's why I don't ever get cocky enough to call myself a "professional."

8

ROAD TRIPS: IT'S THE TRIP, NOT THE RESULT, THAT MATTERS

Hunting is about the kill, but it's the way to the end, and not the end result itself, that is the reason why many of us hunt. Hunting is about the interesting things you learn, the people you meet or get to know, the "you had to be there" things you talk about when you get back home. And it's about the laughs you share in camp. There is all this stuff going on around the actual hunt that is so amazing. On "normal" hunting TV none of it ever gets caught on tape and brought to the viewers. That was our goal with *Road Trips*—to create a different kind of hunting show. *Road Trips* actually got started on a hunt we shot for Realtree Outdoors with Jeff Foxworthy at the Encinitas Ranch.

We had set up a little practical joke for Jeff, who is always bustin' on someone. We got a game warden, who was in on it, to come out and check Jeff's deer, which all of a sudden had "magically" lost its tag. Well, this ole game warden listens to Jeff's story and then politely puts the cuffs on him and arrests him. Jeff is screaming, "You don't understand, this is a mistake! I have my tag! It was on the deer!" We and the game warden went along with it for quite a while and had Jeff pretty worked up, him thinking he was going to jail and all, before we told him it was all a prank.

We all died laughing, but no one thought to film it. The whole week turned out like that: there was funny stuff going on in camp, people were cutting up left and right, but we were just there to get a deer show, so that was all we were filming. Well, one afternoon Steve Finch and I were sitting in the stand and we got to talking about how great it would be to start a new show, one that was shot documentary style and really showed the good times that are had at hunting camp and on the road while hunting. We got more and more excited, bouncing ideas off each other. We were totally oblivious to whether there were any deer coming or not, we were just pumped with the concept for this new show.

We came back and pitched the idea to David Blanton, and, like always, he was supportive of us, but he wasn't willing to put the show on TNN. A couple of years went by and the idea kind of just sat on the back burner, and then one day David came and said, "Guy, go do your show."

"What show?" I responded.

"You know—the one you talked about? The reality show, the one where you host it and Steve films it?"

"That's great! What's the budget?"

"No budget, just work it in under the regular Realtree Outdoors budget."

"Do we get a budget for a graphics package for the intro?" asked Steve.

"Nope."

"What about money for music?"

"Nope, just go do it."

So we went out to film a pilot just Steve and myself. The first trip we went on was to the Gila National Forest in New Mexico for elk. Steve's hope was to just get a show out of this trip. There's nothing worse than conceptualizing a show, then hiking around the mountains for a week and coming home with nothing.

Well, he shouldn't have worried as by the third day we had the makings of a fantastic show—at least a fantastic show that focused on the realities of hunting instead of just the kill. The clouds opened up and it poured on us, we got the truck stuck, got our gear soaked, built a fire, and ate beanie weenies out of a can. Before it was over, we killed a good bull to boot.

With the pilot done, we were off to the races and *Road Trips* was essentially born. While it has evolved over the years, and changed slightly, that basic concept of hunters entertaining hunters has remained the same. As long as we can continue to capture the "why" of the hunt, then it will continue to be successful. In addition to capturing the "why," the other great thing *Road Trips* does is celebrate the hunt with our viewers. We wanted to bring some of the many hardcore hunters from across the United States onto this program and show a little bit of how they do it, share their interesting stories, and in the end sit around the campfire and celebrate our culture together. These shows may have been some of the best we ever did.

Unlike so much of the stuff that is on mainstream TV, we try to bring the good side of "reality TV" to life. In America we have a lot of weird people, but we have a lot more who are honestly good and decent Americans who care about this sport and culture. Those are the people we wanted to showcase.

I think the biggest satisfaction I get from this show is when I really touch a viewer. I can't tell you how many times fans have come up to me at trade shows and told me a story that is shockingly similar to one I have heard before. It generally revolves around how they were watching the show and called to their wife in the other room and made the wife come in and watch. I kept hearing this one common line from all those viewers:

"And I sat her down and said, 'Honey, watch this . . . this is *why I hunt.*'"

Every time a viewer tells me this, I know we have succeeded.

Memorable hunts are the result of many factors. They are not always successful, they are not always exotic, nor are they always focused on a trophy animal. Memorable hunts can come from sharing a unique adventure with family or friends, from seeing a new place for the first time, or from giving something back. While I have said many times that I hunt to kill, sometimes just being there, seeing enjoyment in someone else's eyes is more than enough. The following are those kinds of hunts. They are the ones that stick in my consciousness.

A TURKEY FOR SQUAD 41

One of my most memorable hunts occurred shortly after the tragic events of 9/11.

Squad 41 is a fire department in the South Bronx, in New York City. On 9/11, nearly a whole shift was wiped out when one of the Twin Towers collapsed. Two or three of these guys were hardcore hunters. The squad had sent Realtree.com an e-mail saying what fans they were and how much some of the videos meant to some of the guys in the squad. So we sent them a bunch of DVDs and hats and such. But the more I got to thinking about it, I figured the least I could do to pay tribute and say thanks for the sacrifices they make every day trying to deal with the mayhem of cleaning up the city was to go visit them in person, and let them know we appreciate everything they do. Instead of flying up there, we felt it would only be fitting for the *Road Trips* crew to drive to New York and pick up those guys and take them hunting.

So off we went on a road trip. We drove right into downtown New York City with a big ole jacked-up Chevy pickup truck with a Bad Boy Buggy in the back. The looks we got going through the city were nothing less than incredible! Let me tell you something, 50 Cent, Run-DMC, and LL Cool J all together couldn't have got more attention than we were getting. From the looks on the locals' faces it was obvious they knew the rednecks had come to town.

We finally arrived at the station house and met all the guys from Squad 41. After getting a tour of the firehouse, we got to learn a little about their work, did some practice drills, then took a ride around on one of the fire trucks. It was a fun experience for us, but it made you realize how important, critical, and intense all of their jobs really are. They have to know everything, and when crunch time comes they have to work from instinct.

We spent the evening at the station, where we had one of the best meals I have ever eaten. The firefighters all take turns cooking, and each guy will make his favorite dish, at his own expense. If you want to see competition, drop by Squad 41 around dinnertime. It's like with fast cars, sports, and hunting—guys just have a competitive streak. And for these guys, it was obvious that cooking was no different. Whoever's turn it is to cook does all the shopping and can make anything he wants, but to outdo the other guy, he'll always go full bore, making meals fit for a five-star restaurant. That night we had chicken Alfredo, and I have never had finer . . . anywhere.

After dinner, we relaxed and got to know each other. It didn't take long before we were looking at photo albums of some of the firefighters who died on that horrible day in September. For me that made it real. It was no longer something that was on the news, it was about real people, friends and coworkers.

They were brothers, in every sense of the word. What I saw that night made my blood boil more than it ever has. It made me realize how much the terrorists had really taken away.

While not all of the guys in the squad hunted, some of their fallen brothers had been serious hunters and they realized how important it was in their lives, and I believe some were looking at this trip as part of the healing process. In the end we took Ed Walsh and Jimmy Baranek out for turkeys. We went about an hour and a half away, where there was a good chance at putting the smackdown on some thunder chickens. It was funny—as much as we were fans of them and everything they do, they were equally big fans of us and what we did. In fact, Jimmy and Ed had watched so many Realtree productions that they were real cautious to try to do everything right on camera.

We were on the first stand of the day when right off the bat a gobbler comes struttin' in as if on cue. And when I say "comes in," I mean that joker came right through us, and neither one of the firefighters shot. After the bird was gone, they said, "Did you all get enough footage?" I started laughing. Here I am, wanting to get these guys a bird, and they were so concerned about us getting good pictures. I replied, "Next time just kill 'em. Don't worry, we'll get the footage."

But as so often happens, once you pass up an easy opportunity, things can get tough, and this hunt was no different. We hunted hard with little success. Finally, on the third morning, we yelped a bird in and Ed put out his fire. We were ecstatic now that we had a long-beard on the ground.

But we still had Jimmy's bird to go. So we pulled over to the side of the road to see if we could strike a bird. We got out, called once, and a bird hammered back from the distance. It was showtime. We grabbed our stuff and headed into the woods. As I walked past a lone mailbox I subconsciously took note of the address. We got into the woods, yelped a few times, and got a loud gobble. That old joker was coming on a string. It wasn't but a few minutes and Jimmy killed him clean. We got up, hooting and hollering, happy this hunt was a success. While we were taking some photos, I took a look at my gun. I keep a tally on the rib of my gun of all the birds killed with it that season. With the bird that Jimmy killed, it added up to fourteen. Before I could even think it, Jimmy said, "What is the reverse of fourteen?"

"Forty-one," I answered.

"What was the number on that mailbox?"

"Forty-one," I replied. I was a bit spooked. Squad 41 had had its hunt.

I am not superstitious, but I believe there was a group of firefighters looking out for us that day, hoping their brothers could find some closure in the turkey woods. After seeing the smiles on Ed and Jimmy's faces, I think they did.

BLUE ANGELS

In addition to firefighters and police officers, I have also always had the deepest respect and appreciation for the men and women in our armed forces. They are the backbone of this country. They stand up and protect our values and morals and are the fiber that makes this country great. They are completely unselfish and giving in their devotion to God and country, and I consider it an honor to get to share a hunting experience with them. I have always felt that the soldiers of this country are true heroes. While I have hunted with many military members over the years, one of my most memorable and exciting hunts occurred when I had the opportunity to go into the field with the Blue Angels.

The Blue Angels are, of course, the Navy's elite flying group. They really are the best of the best when it comes to flying. These guys fly at Mach speeds with their wingtips twelve inches apart. Until you have done that, it is hard to describe the amount of skill it takes. Now, there are a lot of great pilots in all branches of

ROAD TRIPS: IT'S THE TRIP, . . . • 97

our military, but the ones who get invited to be a Blue Angel have proven themselves, time and time again, to be among the best of the best. The reason for the existence of the Blue Angels is not only to showcase their talents, but to serve as a recruiting tool for the Navy, which is why I had the opportunity to fly with them.

We were going to fly out of Pensacola, Florida, and when I got down there, it was an amazing experience right from the get-go. Just to meet these incredible individuals, to hear their stories and listen to the things they had seen in battle overseas was a bit overwhelming. As I got to know them, I learned that many of them were also avid hunters, and even though their job may have been different from yours and mine, at their core they were one of us.

While I was looking forward to flying, I was also really looking forward to taking them hunting and giving back to them one tiny little bit of what they give to us every day of the year. As it turned out, Anthony Walley, a Blue Angels pilot, was a serious hunter—but, as I learned from talking to him, he had never killed a turkey. So we took him along with the Blue Angels' chief maintenance officer, Todd Herbert, on down to Magnolia Plantation in Alabama, not far from Pensacola. While everything was shaping up to be a great trip, we only had a day and a half to be with them. So it came down to this: I was going to hunt with Anthony and Todd for a day, then we would get to go fly for a bit. I so badly wanted them to get birds, or at least an opportunity, but at the same time I knew it was going to be tough. The Magnolia Plantation had been hunted a good bit, so these birds had heard calls. It wasn't going to be a slam dunk.

When we got out there, I told Anthony, "You know, turkeys can see real good, so you have to sit extremely still, you can't move. You have to be motionless." Well, the first bird we set up on gobbled good from the roost. Anthony had his gun on his knee, not moving, and I started yelpin' and that turkey flew down. He called back a few times, but then he got henned up and went silent. I knew it was over, but, forgetting that Anthony had never hunted turkeys before, I guess I took it for granted that he knew that bird was henned up and probably wasn't gonna come in, so I didn't say anything to him.

Well, I was pretty tired, as I had been on the road for a while, and I must've dozed off. About twenty minutes later I woke up and Anthony still had his head down on the barrel. He hadn't moved an inch! He was like a statue! That's when I realized I was hunting with a true hardcore soldier. One who took orders and never varied from them. This guy was mentally tough!

Nothing panned out on that setup, but later that afternoon we struck a turkey down on the edge of a food plot, and it was just textbook. The bird sounded off, came in, and Anthony killed it clean. He was so pumped, and I was pumped for him. We were high-fiving and just celebrating like crazy. To have a hunt this short and still close the deal—that made my season.

Well, the following day I got to go flying with the Blue Angels. As long as I live, I don't expect I'll ever feel more exhilarated, excited, or honored than I did that day. The flight itself was one of pure adrenaline, mixed with the gut-churning realization that I might get sick at any moment (I think they wanted me to), but I persevered and kept my lunch down.

Getting to know these true American heroes left me with a feeling of confidence. Not personal confidence, mind you, but confidence in these good, devoted people. These people wake up every morning with AMERICA on their mind. They restored my confidence in where we're heading and who is protecting us. Being a dad, I took from them a feeling of security for the next generation—for my own boys and girl. In short, they made me even more proud to live in America and know that we still are the greatest country in the world.

TRIGGERMAN JOSH

This past spring I met a young man named Josh Olson at the U.S. Army Marksmanship Unit. Josh was shooting on the U.S. Army smallbore team, which is a feat in itself—thousands of excellent riflemen compete for a spot on that team every year. To tell you a little something about the determination and character of Josh: he made the team as an amputee. He had lost one entire leg in Iraq due to an air-to-land missile that hit his Humvee. When I met him, I was on a tour of Fort Benning, Georgia, there to experience the Army Strong program, which allowed me to shoot with the marksmanship squad and skydive with the Army's elite Golden Knight parachute team—an amazing experience. But the highlight of the trip was meeting Josh Olson. We got to know each other, and I invited him to come hunting with me. Like Anthony in the Blue Angels, Josh, though an experienced hunter, had never killed a turkey.

Josh and I went hunting several times, but luck would never shine in our favor and we got skunked every time. Finally I hooked up with my buddy Cory Croft over in Pine Mountain, Georgia. It was the last day of the Georgia season, and it was also Josh's last chance, as he was scheduled to leave that day to go compete overseas. At first light we got on turkeys, but, like every time before, we came close, but no cigar. However, later that afternoon we struck a turkey in a heavily wooded area. We needed to set up quickly

ROAD TRIPS: IT'S THE TRIP, . . . • 101

as this bird sounded hot and was coming in. Josh was making his way down this old logging road, and having a tough time of it. Here is a young twentysomething guy on crutches, on one good leg, having to maneuver over fallen logs and move quietly through heavy leaves. All I could think was, "Wow, this guy lost his leg so we can do exactly what we are doing today. To have the freedom we so enjoy—whether to hunt or fish or just do what we want to do. Thank you, man. Just . . . *thank you.*"

Well, we did get set up, and that turkey came in like clockwork, and while I'd given Josh a lot of instruction on turkey hunting, I musta forgot to tell him to keep his gun over his knee and not to move. So he had his gun lying across his leg, but kinda low. Finally, when the bird got in, he smelled a rat and just took off running full bore, no putt, no nothing. Just full-bore running away. Now, most guys wouldn't have shot, and the few who would've wouldn't have ruffled a feather on that bird, but you probably figured out by now that Josh isn't most guys. He just pulled up like it was any other shot and gave that bird a parking ticket. I can now see why he is on the U.S. Army Marksmanship Unit. The man is an incredible shot.

He was so happy, and he kept thanking me for taking him out, but I'm not sure that he ever realized how sincerely grateful I was for the opportunity, and how thankful I was to him and soldiers like him who have died or been injured in the line of duty.

While I have experienced a lot of memorable hunts with some fantastic individuals, I think that hunt with Josh made the biggest impression on me. It is hard for us to imagine what he went through, lying in some burned-out Humvee in the sandbox of Iraq with his leg blown off. It made me realize all the stuff I take for granted, lying in my own bed in my house or in lodges across this country getting a chance to hunt. Knowing the hell he had been through to ensure we could continue our way of life made me feel kinda small. He paid his dues in full to have the chance to kill this turkey, and I can't tell you how honored I felt just to be there with him and have a chance to experience it and share the story.

9

ELK HUNTING THE WEST

I am proud to know I have some trophy-hunting character in me—the desire to take a buck that scores high on the Boone and Crockett or Pope and Young scale. But I really can't call myself a true trophy hunter, since in reality I just plain like hunting. I love to kill a doe every bit as much as I love to kill a big buck. Yet, at the same time, I do have dreams of taking the biggest specimen of a category. Should I be ashamed of this? No, I don't think so. There is no shame in taking the smartest, oldest, most mature specimen of a species. I think I would become ashamed if I saw overall herd health slipping because of this practice, but it's not. Take a look at the record books for whitetails. Every year the overall size of bucks is getting bigger. Records are continually being broken, which only indicates that because of—not in spite of—trophy hunting we are improving our herd. It is no secret that we are killing more and bigger bucks than two hundred years ago—and probably bigger bucks than existed before Christopher Columbus arrived in America. Hunters' pride in killing mature animals means we are better managing those resources and the habitat that surrounds that resource. For this reason alone there is nothing wrong and everything right with trophy hunting.

Does that mean I just hunt for racks? Heck, no. Take one look in the Waddell freezer right now and you'll see deer, elk, antelope, turkey, but I seriously doubt you'll find even twenty dollars' worth of store-bought meat. My family lives on wild venison. Now, I can't eat everything I kill. I may shoot thirty or forty deer in a year. Some of my biggest trophies I've never even tasted a bite of, but I guarantee you, they never went to waste. Someone ate them. I gave them to friends, family, or donated them to the poor. Nothing ever goes to waste.

The one meat I almost always keep for myself is elk. Elk hunting to me has always been one of the most romantic as well as persistent dreams I had as a boy growing up in Georgia. There weren't any elk running around any of my boyhood hunting grounds, yet they haunted my dreams. I have learned, since growing up and talking to other hunters from all over this great country, that regardless of where you live, if you are a bowhunter, more often than not you dream of someday, somewhere hunting elk with a stick and string.

I vividly remember reading, as a kid, the tales of Fred Bear, Chuck Adams, and Jim Zumbo, all hunting elk in the great Rocky Mountains. I knew even back then that it was just something I had to do. The majesty of elk and their natural surroundings are the icing on the cake. I have always loved to hunt any game that I can interact with and get to come to a call, and elk are possibly the most vocal of all big-game species when the time is right. Combine the lore and mystique with the calling and majestic backdrop, and I simply knew I would love elk hunting years before I actually got to experience it firsthand.

As luck would have it, my first elk-hunting adventure was almost like getting to play in the Super Bowl without ever stepping onto the field. While I wasn't going to get to pull the trigger, or, in this case, release the arrow, I was getting the chance to film with my buddy and boss David Blanton, who had drawn a Unit 7 tag in Arizona. For those who aren't that familiar with Arizona topography, Unit 7 is the Mecca of elk hunting in the West. It has more bulls than most places out West, and more big bulls than nearly anywhere, but getting a tag to hunt the miles upon miles of open ground is almost as hard as actually arrowing an elk. Since it was such a serious hunt for him, and a great opportunity for a big bull, David picked me to be the camera guy because he believed in my hunting ability and with my calling background figured I would be a good guy to have along. Whether I could help or not, he wasn't sure, but he was pretty convinced I represented the best chance to not *mess up* the hunt.

As I mulled the trip over I envisioned riding for miles on horses loaded down with panniers full of gear, or hiking for days with large frame packs to even get where the elk were. But as so often, the reality is far from the dream. Right off the bat, the first morning of the hunt we got out of the truck, walked about a mile, and immediately heard a bull bugle way off in the distance. It was an amazing sound! So we moved in closer and got set up. I set my camera up on a tripod and David tucked in real tight to a small juniper tree. We started calling.

No sooner had the notes left the call but I looked up to see this bull coming across the meadow in front of us. He was coming to the call like he was on a string! I thought, "This setup is a slam dunk. This bull is as good as riding in the back of the truck. All we have to do is figure out what kind of pose we want for the mount." The elk was a monster, realistically a 340-

to 350-class bull, and as big as that is, at the time he looked every bit of 500 inches to me!

By this time in my career at Realtree I had gotten pretty good at filming outdoor television shows, but this bull had me rattled. It was both David's and my first elk hunt, and when my hands went anywhere near the camera I was shaking it. I looked through the viewfinder and could see David's arrow likewise shaking on the rest. Between the two of us, let me tell ya, we were a mess, brother!

That bull kept coming until he was about 35 yards away, but in an attempt to stay out of sight, David had tucked himself so far into the bush that he couldn't get a shot in the direction the bull finally ended up.

Eventually the bull sauntered off, leaving both of us weakened and awestruck. Up until that moment, I only had my own dream of what elk hunting would be like. From then on, I knew that the reality of elk hunting was actually better than the dream, and I was hooked! Elk hunting gave me something different, something that other types of hunting did not. A different rush, a different challenge, a new test to keep my emotions under control, all wrapped up in some of the most wonderful scenery North America has to offer.

I was now hooked on elk hunting, and I hadn't even done it myself yet. I had to get a coveted tag!

It was two years before I would receive a tag and get a chance to play some string music myself. Instead of Arizona, like David, I drew a tag in New Mexico. I was hunting with United States Outfitters on the Floyd Lee Ranch. On the third day of my hunt we managed to call in a great bull. He wasn't a whopper, but he looked to be good enough. As we got him in closer, it was apparent he was a six-by-six in the 270 range, but more than enough to get my blood pumping. We called him all the way in to 10 yards, where I made a perfect shot (at 10 yards it wasn't hard) right through the boiler room. He wheeled and took off, but piled up after leaving a short blood trail. I was ecstatic. I really couldn't have been happier if I had shot a new world record. It was my first bull, and walking up to that wonderful mass of antlers and backstraps was some kind of feeling I'll never forget.

This first bull was an education of sorts for me. I had heard so many stories from guys who had wounded bulls and never found them, or guys who said you couldn't get close enough for a quality shot, that I was seriously worried about drawing my Hoyt back on one. But I realized right there, standing over my first bull, that killing an elk with a bow and arrow is hard, but very possible.

Archery elk hunting does have its own challenges and obstacles. Hunting in the mountains poses the problems of drastically varying thermals from the morning to the evening, which can make or break a stalk. In addition to the challenging wind conditions, elk hunting forces you to get in shape. The more conditioned the better—there is no such thing as "in good shape" when elk hunting. Often you are far into the backcountry and the going can get rough, with lots of steep climbs and treacherous descents. The better shape you are in, the better chance you have of putting your tag on an elk. But in the end, if you have good woods skills, are proficient with your equipment, and hunt the right spots, you can get one.

Elk hunting during the rut is very similar to turkey hunting. Like with David's bull, sometimes you just luck out and get a lovestruck bull to come hammering to the call, but other times, in fact most of the time, you put on miles looking for a bull, and generally when you do find them, just like turkeys, more often than not they are "henned up," surrounded by cows, and only the satellite bulls around the fringes will come in to your call. Unless you draw a tag in an unbelievable trophy unit in Arizona or New Mexico where satellite bulls can be in the mid-300 class, these are generally not the bulls you're after.

After that first bull, I kept on elk hunting as much as possible in as many places as possible. In 2007 I drew a tag for Unit 15 in New Mexico, better known as the Gila National Forest. Since my first bull, I had killed six others with a bow and one with a gun, all on public land except for one. I had previously hunted Unit 15 several times and killed some nice bulls there; in fact, it is one of my favorite units to hunt. So, in 2007 I was hunting with two guides named Andrew and Michael. This particular year there were a lot of big bulls around as it was a wet year, which encourages antler growth through good feed and water. On the first day, we got on a good bull in the 330 to 340 range. He was with several cows and they all bedded just north of a watering hole to wait out the afternoon. The watering hole itself was getting a good bit of activity from elk, so we put up an Ameristep ground blind next to it, figuring the herd might come back in there to water that evening. I set up to wait and see what would happen. In the meantime Andrew and Michael were out scouting, to see if they could locate another bull. I sat on that water hole till dark, but no elk came. It just wasn't my night. Shortly after dark, Andrew and Michael came back and picked me up—and it appeared my luck was about to change.

As soon as I got in the pickup, you could feel the buzz in the air, they were so excited they were about to come unglued. These guys had some nice bull kills under their belts, but they were like a bunch of young-uns they were so excited at what they had seen that afternoon.

"Man, we found two freak nasty bulls," Andrew exclaimed as soon as I got in the truck. There was no debate as to where we were going in the morning— they wanted to chase these bulls. They didn't want my opinion on where to hunt at all. All they wanted to hear from me was that I hadn't shot anything over the water hole. When I told them I did not they said, "Perfect, we are hunting those two big bulls in the morning— no debate about it." If I have learned one thing in all my years of hunting, it is when a guide is excited and shook, you best go for the animal that did the shaking as it will be a monster. Guides see countless animals every year, and it takes a real special animal to get them rattled. Another thing I have learned about experienced western guys is if they say they found a big critter, they generally did. It seems like they are more prone to estimate an animal conservatively than to exaggerate it. Both Andrew and Michael described the bulls they saw as "over 350," so I knew we were talking about super-nice animals. So I just sat there, smiled, and tried to control my guts.

The next morning, we drove into the area, parked the truck, and walked straight up this side hill about 800 yards to a meadow where they were hoping to catch these bulls at first light. This seemed so strange to me, as most other elk hunts I had been on had required hard hunting, days and days of hiking and miles between bulls. This hunt was more like whitetail hunting than the elk hunting I had previously experienced.

When we got up to the meadow it was just breaking light and we immediately saw one bull about a mile away drinking from a watering tank placed in the meadow for the free ranging cattle in the area. He looked good in the dim light but it was hard to tell for sure. As the morning grew lighter we realized the bull was an absolute stud! We heard another bull bugling a half a mile to our right. We glassed in that direction and saw a large group of cows with another bull in the mix.

When the bull at the tank finished drinking, he tipped his head back, bugled once, and started walking toward that bull with the group of cows. We were essentially in between the group of cows and the lone bull at the tank. As he was working his way to the cows, we decided to cut the corner on the distance to put ourselves in range as he walked by. The stalk looked like it was going to work out perfect as we could keep the cows in sight and knew the bull was going to them. As long as we headed toward them we should intercept the bull. The trick was going to be getting far enough ahead of the bull so as to be in place to intercept him when he came by.

We started moving toward the cows, out of sight from the bull. After covering some considerable ground, we heard him bugle again. It was apparent that he had picked up the pace a bit, not because we had spooked him, but just because he was excited to get back to the cows. From the sounds of him, he was getting a better angle on us. So we hurried up a little, now jogging to cut this bull off. When we finally got a glimpse of him again he was slightly in front of us, and had got the angle on us. It looked like he was going to miss us by about 100 yards, too far for a shot. It was just heartbreaking, as now that we could see him better we knew he was not just a good bull but a great one, well over 350 inches.

Well, you never know how an animal is going to react to calling, especially when they already have females around them, but we had to try something or we were going to miss the bull for sure. So Michael started calling to him while we kept stalking. The bull suddenly slowed down. While he didn't come to the call, he did slow down enough that we were able to make up some ground. Michael called again and the bull stopped and turned slightly toward us, but he still didn't commit to coming. About that time right beside us out popped a good 320-class bull. He was enraged and bugling, and had there not been that big guy in front of us I would have just smoked him.

That little bull (only in New Mexico can you call a 320-class bull "little") was our saving grace. The bigger bull turned and started to come toward him. The big bull was now within 70 yards and closing. I got ready for a shot, but couldn't get a range on him so I turned to the guide and asked, "How far is he?" The guide ranged him and said, "He's thirty-seven yards." I looked at the bull and said, "No way is he only thirty-seven yards, he's further than that." It wasn't that I didn't trust my guide, I just knew he was farther away than 37 yards. I am a good judge of distance out to 25 yards, and there was a small tree that I knew was 25 yards away, and this bull was another 20 yards beyond that. So I decided to shoot this bull for the distance I thought he was, which was not 37 yards. In my opinion he was closer to 45 yards. By now the bull had noticed that something was not right. So I drew back and gapped him between my 40- and 50-yard pins. I took my time and squeezed the trigger.

The arrow launched toward the bull. I watched it arcing, and arcing, and I am thinking, "Hammered him!" but then the bottom starts dropping out of it and my thoughts switched from making touchdown signs to hanging my head in disappointment. I remember thinking, "Oh no, I'm gonna miss him, he was further than what I thought." Then the bull saw the arrow coming. And what did he do but drop down in order to take off running—when the arrow hit him. He dropped right into it. The bull turned to wheel out of there and I noticed he was hitting his brisket on the ground, with both front legs churning. From past experience that is a sign of a dead animal. If you put an arrow in one side and it damages the off-side foreleg, you generally put it through something meaty and juicy that their body doesn't like to lose.

He finally got out of there, and we waited a bit before going out to where I shot him. It turned out he had been 53 yards away. I misjudged him by nearly 10 yards. We rewound the footage and saw how through a stroke of God's grace this bull had ducked the string and ducked right into my arrow. Had he not done that, I would have missed him by at least twelve inches. If I had shot for the correct distance, 53 yards, I more than likely would have shot right over the top of him when he dropped to run.

Not knowing how good the shot was, we waited an hour before going after him. When we did start blood-trailing him, we hadn't gone far when we spotted him. I put up my binoculars and saw him down, getting ready to die, and I did as any good Georgia redneck would do. I slipped up a little closer and put two more arrows into his boiler room at 45 yards.

The arrows were nearly touching. He didn't move, he just died right there.

Well, if I have ever come close to making out with a man, it was never as close as that day. The two guides and I were high-fiving, hugging, and knocking each other down. We were all just totally pumped to see this monster on the ground. We thought he would go 360, but as we walked up to him, he just kept growing and growing. It turns out he was the bull the local outfitters and guides had been referring to as the "Professor," owing to he was so smart and call shy. Well, I have always said I would rather be lucky than good, and my luck was running high that day; in fact, I should have gone right out and bought a lottery ticket as here we were with the Professor down on the second day of the hunt. Another great stroke of luck occurred when we were able to drive the truck to the bull so we didn't have to quarter him up and pack him out. We got him back to camp and he ended up scoring 378 inches! He was one huge six-by-six, with tons of mass and tine length. There is hardly any place where you can reach around them.

An interesting side note to this bull came about when we took him to the processor. The butcher who ended up splitting him in half came out and handed me an arrow and said, "Here is your arrow back."

I said, "No, I already have my arrows."

"Well, this arrow was in him."

This bull had a complete shaft inside of him. The arrow was completely within his rib cage, high, just below the spine. It looked like it had been there for a year or so. I am sure that some other hunter tells stories of the big one he hit and never found. While it is unfortunate to lose an elk that you hit pretty well with an arrow, it is good to know that this bull healed up and was doing just fine.

Speaking of strange elk stories, I have another one that is a bit strange, but to me very comforting. I was again hunting the Gila in New Mexico with Perry Hunsaker. I was frustrated, coming off a Wyoming hunt at the Wagon Hound Ranch. It was a good hunt, but we had gotten snakebit by the wind and thermals. Every time I would get a shot opportunity at a really big bull, the wind would shift and it would blow my opportunity. To make a long story short, I got skunked there and headed straight to New Mexico for a public-ground hunt in the Gila. It was a good year in the Gila, where they'd had plenty of rain and there were lots of really nice bulls running around. And it looked as if my luck was going to turn around, as we were on them. By the third day of the hunt, we had more encounters than you could shake a stick at, but just like in Wyoming the wind would end up screwing us, or we couldn't get them away from the cows, or there was always just something they didn't like. There is nothing more frustrating than being close, time and time again, without letting an arrow fly.

Finally, on the third day we had a good bull working. He was bugling and circling around us and we kept working him, playing cat and mouse. Finally, after a couple of hours, we thought we had him. He was down below us in this bottom and we were above him on this ridge and he started coming up the mountain toward us. We had a steady wind blowing in our face—it was all too perfect. This bull was coming up the ridge, working along a trail that would lead him right to us. I grabbed my rangefinder and ranged a tree that was 50 yards, then I ranged another one closer along the trail that was at 42 yards. I knew if he kept coming up that trail he would be between those two trees. Well, he kept bugling and sure enough he eventually got to the 42-yard tree. When his head went behind a tree I came to full draw, but as soon as I did I felt the wind shift and hit me on the back of the neck. The bull immediately started to turn to go back down the hill. But since I was drawn back and knew the range I took the shot. The arrow hit the bull in mid-turn, entering at about his liver, but a bit high. Even though the shot wasn't perfect, I felt that it was good enough to get one if not two lungs as it ranged forward and down into his chest cavity. There was little doubt in my mind that I just killed this bull, but just to be sure we gave him an hour or so before we started tracking him. We hadn't gone very far when we jumped a bull. I didn't know if it was our bull or a different one, but he went up the ridge. If you know anything about wounded animals, you know this was not a good sign.

At this point we decided to pull out and leave the bull for a while, to avoid pushing him into the next county. When we got back down to the old Forest Service road, Perry said, "Why don't we go back to camp, eat a hot lunch, and get some help. We can all come back in several hours and see if we can't find this bull."

I said, "You know what, Perry, I have been around a lot of people lately. Why don't you all go back and round up some guys. I think I'm just gonna sit here, relax, eat my sack lunch, and take a nap."

So they left and I lay there under a tree, thinking about that bull. I knew he was dead and I was aggravated we couldn't find him. So after a couple of hours of tossing and turning and not being able to take a nap, I got up and started walking along the Forest Service road. I walked down through this big pine bottom, just looking around, enjoying the environment, and said under my breath, "Daggum it, Momma, I know that bull is dead. You need to show me where he is." Now, this is something I have never done before or since, but it just felt right to ask my deceased mother for help at that time.

I immediately look up and I saw this red Chevy pickup parked off to the side of the Forest Service road. Looking through my binoculars I could see the truck had New Mexico plates and a Team Realtree sticker on the back window. Obviously these guys were out hunting, so I decided I would walk over to the truck and leave my business card with a note saying I wounded an elk in this area, if they happened to stumble across it please give me a call. So I reached into my pack, looking for any business card I might have. When I looked up, there was a bull elk walking right behind the truck. And I mean right behind! This joker wasn't 19 yards behind the bumper, heading toward the road. He had his head slung low and you could tell he wasn't well. But there was no way that it could be my bull. We had just seen him going up a ridge in the opposite direction from this road, in an area I guessed to be a couple of miles away.

Still, it did look like my bull. I couldn't see the side I shot and he was walking right toward me. When I looked through my binoculars again at the rack I immediately knew it *was* my bull. He was now about

90 yards away. A peace settled over me as I just knew . . . It was like I had a guardian angel on my shoulder.

He kept walking at a steady but slow pace, so I pulled out my rangefinder and ranged him. He was 79 yards away. I pulled up and looked to see if there was a shot opportunity, but there was a downed tree about 40 yards out, lying in the way of the bull's vitals. I hesitated to shoot for fear of hitting the tree before it dawned on me the arrow would arc well over the tree and have a clear flight. So I cow-called to him and he completely stopped. I drew back, put my 80-yard pin on him, and the arrow went over the tree and just hammered him.

As soon as I released the arrow, all the confidence and security I had knowing this was my bull disappeared. Now I was full of self-doubt. I walked over and sat by a tree and thought to myself, "Oh boy, I hope I just didn't kill two elk." I was between nervous and excited. On the one hand, I was worried that it wasn't my elk, but on the other, I was also elated as it was the best shot I had ever made.

It wasn't long afterward that Perry and the crew came back. They parked the truck and were getting their stuff ready to go on up the mountain to look for my bull and I pulled our cameraman Mark Womack aside and hissed, "Mark, I need to tell you something. I know you are going to think I am crazy, but I think I just shot my bull again." He looked at me like I was smoking something. "Dude, your bull should be no-where around here. You just shot another bull."

"I might have. But before we go tell everyone else, I need you to go look for me."

I am lousy at blood trailing because I am color-blind, so I took Mark over behind the truck to see if there was blood. Now, I knew there would be blood in *front* of the truck, which is where I smoked that bull; but I had to know if I made a mistake or not, and the only way to know for sure before we started following up that bull was to see if there was blood in the area before I shot. We got over there and Mark didn't walk 10 yards before he said, "Blood! Right here!" Relief swept over me like a wave and I called Perry over to me and told him the story. We walked over there and found my arrow and it was covered in blood. We went another 70 yards and there lay the bull. Walking up to it, it was easy to see it was my bull.

What are the chances of that happening? Usu-ally I would have ridden back to camp with them and wouldn't have even been in the woods when the bull came through. And why did he walk right around a parked pickup, and why did he appear almost imme-diately after I asked my momma for help? I don't have the answer to these questions. I just know that even though my mother left me physically when I was sixteen, she is with me every time I hunt. There is not a shadow of a doubt about that.

It's funny, but I grew up dreaming about how difficult elk hunting would be, and in many instances my dreams have been correct. Steep mountains, long hikes, and heavy loads make for tough going, but hunting for the biggest bull of my career may have possibly been the easiest elk hunt I ever went on or will ever go on again. It is amazing to think that there are still places in this great country of ours where you can find a bull of this caliber on public land and get him within two days of hunting. It just goes to show that being in the right place at the right time and doing your homework can put you in the position to take a trophy bull. It also goes to show that no matter how much you prepare and practice and hone your ability to close the coffin, things don't always go as planned and luck can always play a big role.

Elk hunting is one of America's great conservation success stories. As with turkeys, which have been successfully reestablished throughout much, if not all, of their historic range, elk numbers are likewise at a fifty-year high. There is no better time than the present to head west to fulfill those boyhood fantasies. I know this country boy from Booger Bottom will return every year he's lucky enough to draw a tag.

10

MULE DEER ADDICTION

It's funny how some animals rank really high on a hunter's list while others don't. It is also interesting how the ranking of animals can change drastically over the years as a hunter changes and experiences different things. Mule deer have been this type of animal for me over the years. Mule deer were never something I really dreamed of hunting and if you asked me a dozen years ago to rank my "dream" animals, mule deer wouldn't have placed very high. Now, after experiencing them in several states, they are one of my favorite animals to hunt every year.

My first experience with mule deer really began when I was looking for whitetails in Kansas on a Unit 2 muzzleloader tag. This tag was good for either a mulie or a whitetail, but the reason I was excited about going to Kansas was to hunt big whitetails. Well, after I got out there, I was informed by the outfitter that they didn't really have any impressive whitetails, but they had some good mule deer.

"I was actually looking forward to hunting whitetails . . . but what's a really nice mule deer around here?" I asked.

"Well, we have one that will go over two hundred inches and another that will go over a hundred and eighty inches," the outfitter replied.

Hearing this changed my opinion of mule deer in Kansas, so I said as casually as I could, "Okay, that will actually be just fine."

So we took off after mule deer, and on the first day of the hunt we started walking over the first ridge, less than 300 yards from the pickup. When we got to the top we peeked over the ridge and saw a group of does. And right there, off to one side of the does, was that big ole buck they had been seeing. My luck appeared too good to be true.

My luck, however, was not perfect. He was 200 yards away. While 200 yards isn't that far, keep in mind I was hunting with a muzzleloader. I did have a scope on it, because in the late season you could use a scope on a muzzleloader, but it is still a muzzleloader, and 200 yards is just too far of a shot with a smokepole, regardless of your sights.

The country was super open, but we tried to stalk this buck anyway. This was just plain tough, especially with a camera following behind. There wasn't a blade of grass or cover between us and them. We blew the first stalk, but the deer didn't go all that far, so we thought we might get another chance. Well, we blew it again, and again, as we kept trying to get within range of this buck. We were getting very nervous because even though we were on private property, at every fence corner where our property ended there were trucks waiting for that buck to step over the line. Bucks of this size don't go unnoticed anywhere, and in open country like western Kansas they always get discovered sooner or later. The word had definitely got out that this big ole boy was in the country, and ranchers and other hunters on adjacent property were just waiting for him to pay a visit to their land.

This game of blowing stalk after stalk went on all day. It looked like we weren't going to get a shot at this buck, but right before dark we slipped up along this ridge and daggum, there he stood at 130 yards. I knew it was now or never, so I steadied my T/C and squeezed the trigger. Across the distance I heard the bullet hit and I knew I cracked him solid. He didn't go far before piling up. Talk about getting lucky! My first mule deer hunt, the first mule deer I had ever *seen*, and I had a 200-inch deer down on the ground. It is no wonder why I got addicted to mule deer hunting!

Obviously my early success on mule deer made it easy to love hunting them, but there is more to it than that. The difference between whitetail hunting and mule deer hunting is huge, and, to be honest, mule deer hunting fits my style of hunting much better. It is no secret that I am not the most patient person walking the planet. As any whitetail hunter knows, to be successful on trophy whitetails you have to be patient. Whitetail hunting generally involves sitting in a stand all day, by yourself, remaining motionless, waiting for something to come by. It is hours of solitary boredom punctuated with a few seconds of intense action. Unless the deer are running hard, it is difficult for me to do this day after day. But when you are hunting for mule deer, you are always doing something. And there is so much camaraderie involved with it. You get to talk, you get to enjoy friends, and it gives you an opportunity to stalk game. There is little downtime. It's all about making a plan, and then executing that plan. I love that type of hunting. Mule deer hunting lends itself well to my hunting abilities. Typically you have to be prepared to make longer shots, which is something I practice heavily for and am confident about. For archers, this means being able to make 40-yard-plus shots in field conditions.

Muzzleloader hunters should be able to reach out a mite past 100 yards.

I am often asked at sports shows, and hunting seminars, or just by fans, how far should archers be shooting at game. This is probably one of the most argued topics in the hunting community—what is the effective range of a bow and arrow and how ethical is it to shoot at game at the outer limits of this range? Well, the reason it is so debated is because there really is no right answer. Like many things in the hunting world, there is no blanket statement that says 40 yards is okay but 43 yards is completely wrong. It is just not that simple. So much goes into taking a shot. The conditions that day, the awareness of the animal, the species of animal, the type of equipment being used, and the proficiency of the hunter.

On a calm day with no wind and good light, it is a lot easier to make a shot than on a dark, overcast day, or in those last few minutes of daylight when the wind is blowing a gale, and the hunter is cold and shaky. Also consider the type of animal being hunted. A whitetail, especially an old mature buck that is jacked up, has a much quicker reaction time than an elk in a limited-draw unit, or a caribou up north that rarely sees people. What this means for the bowhunter is that even if you can hit the target at a given range, that animal may not be standing there when the arrow arrives. This "jacked-upness" even varies among animals of the same species. In heavily hunted areas, or when it is super-cold and sound carries well, such as on a late-season hunt, a particular animal may be much more alert than he would be earlier in the season or if there was a slight breeze rustling the leaves. This is where a hunter's experience can also play a part in success. Having an educated guess at what a particular animal's reaction is going to be determines how far you should be shooting.

It was easy to find myself going on another mule deer hunt. After Kansas, my next adventure came about in southeastern Colorado. While I had never hunted there before, I was soon to find out that the open plains of Colorado are fun hunting. It is big country. It is open prairie with some creek bottoms, some crops, and some huge mule deer. My first trip there came about several years ago when my good buddy and country music artist Rhett Akins and I went out there to hunt with Aaron Neilson of Adventures Wild. From the time we arrived it was obvious Aaron had a banger of a spot. We got on big deer after big deer, spotting and stalking. We even got on some great whitetails and came close to tagging some, but the problem with big whitetails in that country is they are so hard to spot and stalk. You will get within range of one in its bed, but when they blow out, they BLOW OUT, son! Unlike a mule deer, which will jump up, stand for a second to see what disturbed him, and so give you a shot, when a whitetail decides to leave, he is gone, making spot-and-stalk hunting with a bow extremely difficult.

After blowing several stalks on both mule deer and whitetail, on the second day of the hunt Rhett missed a monster! He was a 170-inch-plus deer for sure. He missed it at 30 yards. Rhett is still convinced he shot a dud arrow, but I suspect he picked the wrong pin or just didn't settle his pins. A buck of that size will make you do funny things. But all things happen for a reason. We hunted for a couple more days, passed up some deer, blew some more stalks, and Rhett ended up killing a 180-inch deer!

No sooner had Rhett got his deer down but we found a bruiser that the guides had been looking for. Evidently they had put several stalks on him with other clients, and one client had shot and missed him, so this buck was a bit jacked up and aware of the program. He was with some does when I decided to put a stalk on him. Well, before I could get in range, the does busted me and blew out, taking the buck with them. We kept stalking him, and just before dark we caught back up

Killing a big old gobbler, especially in the South, is probably one of the most challenging and frustrating things you can do. But it keeps us all coming back for more.

Thunder chicken down!

I love hunting turkeys so much because you can talk to them. Learning to master a call is an art in itself that is thoroughly enjoyable.

After days of getting into the backcountry, and just hard hunting, I managed to smoke this moose with one arrow, to the surprise of Rhett Akins and the guide.

We rushed to get Rhett's bull out of the backcountry in time to meet our bush flight home, only to get socked in with weather and stuck in camp.

Antelope hunting with a bow and arrow can either be extremely easy or require a long wait in a sweltering ground blind. Most of the time, it is the latter.

Caribou hunting is a great time: there are lots of animals, it is a wild adventure, and best of all you get to share it with a group of buddies.

A man has got to find something to do in the off-season, right? Grab a bow and some fish arrows, and see what bow fishing is all about.

If you ever get the chance, go hunt elk. The reality is often even better than the dream. With bulls like this roaming public land, I go back as often as possible.

No matter what else I do in life, no matter where in the world I hunt, the good old American whitetail will always captivate me.

Another whitetail that was dying to become a movie star on *Road Trips*.

I absolutely love chasing mule deer in the West. This old joker came out of one of my favorite spots in Colorado.

Top: The next generation of Waddell hunters: my boy Mason with some ducks our group shot one morning. Even at an early age, he is torn up with passion for the sport.

Center: Rhett and I playin' some oldies in camp. I am sure it was something by Hank Williams, Jr.

Below: This was one of the most fun hunts I can remember. Good hunting combined with good friends like Rhett Akins, Mark Womack, and T-Bone Turner.

My boy Mason is following in the Waddell clan tradition of hunting and shooting from an early age.

With eyes like that, when Mason ain't breaking targets he will be breaking gals' hearts. But maybe I am just biased.

While hunting takes a lot of my time, when I am home, I enjoy just spending time with the kids watching them grow up.

Nothin' better than Women Gone Wild. In this case it is Tiffany Lakosky, Kandi Kisky, and my wife, Ashley.

Nothing like sharing a camp with good friends like T-Bone and Lorrie Morgan.

What a hunt, what a hunt! Getting to share camp with Uncle Ted and Blake Shelton is an experience in itself.

Africa is a land of opportunity with more animals than I can name. Whether you go for elephants or an impala like this one, it is an experience that shouldn't be missed.

The workin' man's Cape buffalo: the blue wildebeest. This old joker came into the water hole, and even though I wasn't an Africa expert, I knew enough to realize he was a shooter!

with him. He was now bedded down on a sage flat. The wind was howling. We crept up to within 15 yards of him. I knew he was right in front of me and I could see the tops of his heavy, tall antlers occasionally sticking up, but he wouldn't stand up or present a shot. I grunted at him, trying to get him to stand up, but it was so windy I doubt he could hear me. I drew back to full draw and grunted louder. This time the buck heard me, but unlike most mule deer, this cagey old joker busted from his bed like a whitetail at full tilt. As soon as he started to lunge, I released the arrow. He was severely quartering away and the arrow went in right in front of the hip and came out the brisket. He went about 60 yards before he bought a piece of Colorado real estate.

Walking up to him, I knew this was the buck of my dreams. While guys talk about ground shrinkage, and I have experienced it myself, a truly big buck just keeps getting bigger in those last steps up to him. By the time I got up to him, I was elated. He went 187 3/8, which is an excellent buck by any method, but a complete monster with a bow.

More than just the fun of mule deer hunting, what I really enjoy is the country and the people of the West. This is completely remote, rural country where a man can sit on one hill and look literally for miles without seeing a building, a road, or another person.

The western people are also unique. They are hard-working folks, getting up early every day to farm or ranch, never asking nothing from nobody.

After hunting Kansas and Colorado I decided to give Montana mule deer a try with a rifle. What was cool about that hunt is that it was a different type of hunt than I had previously experienced. Deer were hitting alfalfa fields and then going up into the coulees to bed. This type of regularity, especially combined with a rifle tag, made for some exciting hunting. We could spot and stalk or just wait, as all of the deer in the area would eventually come back into the fields to feed in the evening. We had seen this one particular buck several times, though, and we decided we would go for him. He wasn't a monster like I had been lucky enough to get in Kansas and Colorado, but he was a nice Montana buck that would go 150 to 160 inches. The deer's movements were pretty predictable, as he was working through a particular draw to get to the alfalfa field.

We moved in early and set up an Ameristep ground blind to try to catch him as he came through. The problem with hunting from an ambush spot out West is that the country is so big, it is hard to pick exactly where the deer may come, even when you have them patterned. But we figured that even if the deer missed us, we could always slip out of the blind and put a stalk on him out on the alfalfa flat.

It wasn't long before we started to see some deer moving. Then a group of does started down that draw. The buck was with them. Before we knew it, the buck was angling right toward us, working into range all the time. Mark Womack was filming this hunt for an episode of *Road Trips*, and he was getting some great footage of this buck as he worked his way to us. All of a sudden the buck cut to the right and Mark had to pick the camera and tripod up in the blind and re-position it to keep the buck on camera. I didn't think much about it, as Mark is a pro who never, and I mean never, misses a shot with a camera; but this time he did. Unbeknownst to either of us, he accidently hit the stop button, shutting the camera off. (Looking through the viewfinder, you could still see the deer, but in the excitement, Mark didn't notice it didn't say "record.") After he framed up the deer in the viewfinder, he told me to shoot. So I shot this buck with my T/C Encore and he piled up. I don't know who was more shocked, Mark or me, when it came time to review the footage. It was one of very few times in his career that Mark has missed a shot.

My mule deer hunting experience, while relatively lim-ited, has been unbelievably blessed. The last mule deer hunt I went on was no exception. I returned to Colorado to hunt again with Aaron Neilson, and this time we were hunting over some big cut cornfields in November. It was a different type of mule deer hunting than I had previously experienced in Colorado. The rut was still on, and deer were grouped up around the available food sources. We started glassing from the pickup, and it wasn't long before we spotted a great buck feeding out in the middle of one of these cornfields. He was not an average or even a good buck—he was a great buck. After looking him over, we decided he probably would go over 200 inches. The problem was, he was not stalkable at all. The cornstalks were short, and he was with a bunch of does. Getting to him would require moving unseen over a mile, with nothing to hide behind. So, with a disappointed sigh, we just kept on driving, looking for another buck in a better location. Not seeing anything that came even close to that first buck, we returned to that spot a little later, hoping he had moved off into a more accessible area. But he hadn't. He was now bedded down right in the middle of that cornfield with twenty-five or so does. Even though we knew it was a lost cause, we looked over every possibility of a stalk again. The highest stalk of corn was twelve to fifteen inches. No brush, no fence line, no nothing. Just a big field of corn. This was a job for a rifle, not a bow. After looking it over one more time, we all agreed it was impossible. All of us had done enough hunting to know that this kind of situation is just a waste of time. You'll spend hours trying, and never get within range. But we kept looking at that massive buck, and I thought to myself, "How can you not at least *try* and stalk a 200-inch deer. Even if I spook him, it will be worth it just to try." So finally, around eight thirty in the morning, we decided to go after him and started stalking through this corn flat.

The field appeared as flat as a pancake, but upon closer examination there was one little swale, and the deer were right on the other side of it. It wasn't much, but maybe it was enough to make a difference. So for over a mile we crawled, literally on our bellies, in the depression of this swale. It was a super-slow process. Face flat to the ground, you would slide your bow in front of you, then grab the earth with your fingers and push with your toes to gain a few inches, only to repeat the performance. Finally, at four o'clock in the afternoon we were almost within range of this buck. It was unbelievable! We were tired and frozen. We had been giving it everything we had, all day long. We could see the light at the end of the tunnel and had actually started to find some hope in this impossible situation—when all of a sudden the group of deer gets up and starts walking away from us. They weren't spooked, they were just changing locations. So we picked up the pace to keep up with them. They didn't go far before bedding back down. Slowing back down, we kept crawling toward them, keeping that big buck in view all the time.

All of a sudden we get up on a young buck, between us and the big buck. This was now a problem. I checked some distances with my Bushnell rangefinder and realized that in order to even get within 60 yards of the big buck I was going to have to sneak within 20 of this young buck. So I kept crawling, and before I knew it, I was within 20 yards of the young buck. Thinking to myself, "It's now or never," I rose up and got in position to draw.

The young buck sees me do this and stands up, looking right at me. He is literally burning holes in me with his eyes, but since the wind is blowing in our faces he walks past us in a spooked semicircle, looking at us the whole time but never putting the whole picture together. Now the does see that this young buck is alerted, so they stand up, looking at the little buck, all their senses on edge. Well, the little buck walks quartering past us, and the does follow. The big buck knows something is not right, so he stands up, looking at the does and the smaller buck, and starts walking after them. The big buck stops for a second and I get a range on him at 57 yards.

It was a tough shot, slightly quartering to, with does all around him. I had to shoot a perfect shot, in the wind and cold after I had been lying on the ground all day long. It was a thread-the-needle situation, but it was now or never, so I drew back, settled the pin, and squeezed the trigger. The arrow left the bow, and I followed its flight with my eyes, watching the arrow disappear into his chest. I hammered him! He didn't go far before piling up. I was just elated. But it was an emotional drain, along with a sense of tremendous accomplishment, doing what we thought we couldn't do. When we walked up to him, there was no ground shrinkage. He scored 200 inches, on the nose. He was just a giant of a deer, and one that taught me a lot about stalking.

It just goes to show, you can never throw in the towel in any situation. No matter how impossible something looks, you really never can know how it will turn out unless you give it an honest try. If you get an opportunity, there is always hope. If you execute with all of your hunting skills, you can be successful, even in the most adverse conditions.

I have been very lucky on mule deer. In this day and age, killing big mule deer is tough, just because there aren't many of them. Unlike with whitetails, which seem to keep getting bigger every year, trophy mule deer hunting is not what it was twenty-five or so years ago. Many of the big bucks are no longer around. Habitat encroachment by whitetails, hunting pressure, and land development has seriously hurt them, so I consider myself very fortunate to have taken what I have. I haven't killed a lot of mule deer—only four—but they have all been great bucks. A 160-, a 187-, and two 200-inch deer. Two with a bow, one with a muzzleloader, and one with a rifle. Mule deer have been the highest-quality animals per hour spent chasing of any animal I have hunted in North America.

One place I haven't hunted mule deer but would really like to is up in Alberta. I hear there are monster mule deer there. New Mexico, Nevada, and Arizona also rate high on my list of places to hunt before it is all over. That country is full of monster mule deer with great genetics. Randy Ulmer, a competitive archer and hero of mine, has killed some magnificent deer out there in Nevada. Hopefully, one of these days I will head the pickup in that direction and give the gray ghosts of the West another go.

11

NORTH TO ALASKA

When I was younger, if I had made a list of all the things I wanted to do in the hunting field it would have included elk hunting, hunting a brown bear or grizzly with a bow, hunting a Cape buffalo (of course), and hunting a big Alaskan moose with a bow. In a nutshell, those were all of my "exotic" big-game goals.

While I had wanted to do an Alaskan hunt for quite some time, even when opportunities arose I just kept pushing them off, as it is not a cheap trip. Even when an outfitter donates his portion of the trip, there is still the cost of getting to Alaska, getting meat and horns home, buying licenses, and chartering flights on small planes. No matter how you slice it, Alaska is just an expensive place to visit. So if you are going to do Alaska, with all the costs involved, it better be the stuff that dreams are made of.

Well, finally, after several years of not finding exactly what we were looking for, we learned of Terry Overly's Pioneer Outfitters. After we did a bit of research, they appeared to offer just what we wanted. They prided themselves in retro-style Alaskan trips, using horses to get you way back in the country, where you roughed it. No fancy lodges, few modern improvements, but Alaska—raw, pure, and simple, the way early hunters would have experienced it. And that was exactly what we were looking for.

When we started planning for this trip and brainstorming some ideas, we remembered Elmendorf Air Force Base and thought it would be cool to get up there and hunt with some of the soldiers. Some of the soldiers, in turn, thought it would be great if I could get a country music singer to come on up with me and put on a concert at the base. So I invited Rhett Akins to come along on the adventure.

The plan was to go up there at the end of September. Rhett and I would both hunt moose and bear in the Wrangell Mountains. We were to hunt for ten days, then go back to Elmendorf Air Force Base, where Rhett would put on a concert. Sounded like a simple enough plan, but, as we were soon to learn, Alaska doesn't always go along with your plans.

Stepping off the plane in Anchorage, I was simply blown away by the beauty of the country, the sheer size and vastness of it combined with the rugged majesty of the mountains. But one thing that surprised me when we got afield was that there was not nearly as much game just walking around as I had anticipated.

We spent some time hunting around Anchorage with some soldiers just to see if we could rustle up a bear, but after a couple days of no luck, we decided it was time to head into the backcountry, to Terry Overly's base camp. Getting to Terry's jumping-off point was a bit of an adventure in itself. In the Lower 48 you can generally just drive to camp. Not so with most places in Alaska. We started at a small airstrip (which was itself a six-hour drive from Anchorage) where Terry met us in his small black plane. Loaded to the hilt with gear, we took off for Terry's main camp, which was also his year-round residence (a bit off the beaten path, to say the least).

When we finally got to Terry's camp, we discovered we were going to have a girl guide named Amber. No problem there. We figured if she was tough enough to be living in the bush in Alaska, she was tough enough to guide us. Since it was late in the evening when we finally got there, we weren't going to head out until the next day. The plan was to get up the next morning, shoot our guns and bows, repack our gear into horse panniers, and head out around one o'clock on horse-back, as we had a thirty-mile ride into the spike camp.

So the next morning we got up and had a nice break-fast. During breakfast it was hard to miss that Terry Overly had a penchant for black. Everything the man owned was black. His plane was black, the plate he ate breakfast off of was black, as was his fork and the clothes he wore—all black. He was a combination of Dale Earnhardt and Johnny Cash—he was the Alaskan Man in Black.

I had figured that after breakfast we would shoot the rifles, check the bows, and head out, but then . . . nothing really happened. We just sat around talk-ing. Pretty soon it was one o'clock, then two o'clock, and then Terry said, "Well, it's getting pretty late, we'll just go tomorrow." This took me aback, and I realized right then and there that we were in a differ-ent time zone—Alaskan time. There was no pressure, no rush. In fact, I believe a lot of the slowdown was on purpose, to get hunters to relax, to get back to the reason why they came in the first place. In our modern world everything is goal oriented, pressure induced, and on a rigid timeline. Terry was the antithesis of all that. His first goal was to get hunters to shed those trappings—out at his cabin there was no town, no cell service, really no way back to civilization—and to reset our mental clocks to "hunting time." In other words, you would go hunting when Terry said you would go hunting.

Come the next morning, I figured we would get up early, have a quick breakfast, and hit the trail. But the second day was a carbon copy of the first day. We got up, ate a big breakfast, and then sat around talking. It wasn't until about three in the afternoon that we actually got on the horses for our ten-hour ride to camp.

For the first mile or two it was the most unbelievable thing in the world. We were just riding along, gawking at the mountains, fording glacial rivers, seeing eagles flying over us—everything about it was pure Alaska. It was everything I had expected and more.

After a couple of hours of this scenic overload, while still amazing, the novelty began to wear off. Eventually our butts got so sore that we had to get off the horses and walk with them. After hours of riding and walking, we finally saw tents off in the distance. Finally we were at our spike camp! We rode up to the tents, and the assistant guide jumped off his horse. Not saying anything, he started tearing the tents down!

"What are you doing?" I said. "We're finally here."

In typical quiet Alaskan fashion, he responded, "No, this isn't camp. We are halfway there. This is just an old camp I am tearing down for the season."

I looked at Rhett and he looked at me. The expression in both of our eyes told the tale—we were both deflated. I don't think we could have been any lower. We were both somewhere between laughing and crying, but the only thing to do was saddle up and keep riding.

About two hours before we got to our real camp it got pitch-black dark. Riding through the darkness, we saw the white tents in the distance and our moods improved dramatically.

Rhett exclaimed, "There's the tents! There's the tents!" He was freaking out, making the touchdown sign. He was more than ready to get off the horse, eat a meal, and bunk down at camp.

Well, when we got up to the "tents," we realized it was just a snowbank—no tents. We still had a ways to go.

It was another hour or so on the trail before we finally got to camp. In all, there were seven of us in our party: Rhett, myself, Ron Nemetchek (hunting buddy and guide from Canada), and Steve Finch as well as guides Amber, Brian, and Spencer. When we got to camp, there was one small, little cabin, maybe twelve by fifteen foot. It had small, little hockey-glass windows to keep the bears out, a little kitchen area, some bunks, and a potbelly stove for warmth. Amber had started carrying her stuff inside, so we followed suit, unloading our personal gear and stowing it in the cabin. Before we could get much unloaded, she turned and said, "Um, you all need to go get your tent set up."

Looking at the extra bunks in the cabin, I said, "I thought we would all be staying in here."

"No no no. Typically the guides and clients all sleep in here, but since I am a gal, I am sleeping in here and all of you are sleeping outside."

"Well, that sure isn't worth a pinch of coon shit right there," I remember thinking as I walked back outside. So we set up one wall tent for Rhett, myself, Ron, and cameraman Steve Finch, while the guides set up two smaller pup tents for themselves. There was deep snow on the ground and it was cold—not exactly my idea of camping weather! Now, I have no problem with a woman being a guide, but she needed to realize we were there to hunt, nothing else, and all of us staying in the same warm cabin shouldn't have been a problem.

The next morning we slept a bit late, since we got in so late the night before. After we got up and got a fire going, we had to wrangle the horses, which had been hobbled but still managed to cover some territory before we found them. By the time everything was ready to go hunting, it was one o'clock in the afternoon. With the horses all saddled up, we headed afield and traveled into the hunting territory. We hunted the rest of the day but didn't have much to show for it, except for one cow moose we saw on a distant hillside as the sun was going down.

The following day was much the same, and each successive day started rolling into a similar pattern. We would get up, collect the horses, head afield, hear or see a moose, but never get close enough to get a shot with a bow. We would then return to camp, eat dinner, play the guitar a bit, then roll into our cold sleeping bags for an uncomfortable night of fitful sleep. We quickly realized that neither Rhett nor I really had the right sleeping bags for this type of trip. Rhett had gotten a cheap sleeping bag with little insulation, and my sleeping bag turned out to be mislabeled. I thought it was a minus-40 bag, but really it was a plus-40 bag meant for summer camping. In any case, both of us froze at night and were miserable. We had a small woodstove inside our tent, but soon after we nodded off, the logs would burn down and the temperature would immediately plummet. We were forced to sleep with all our clothes on, and we were still freezing cold. It was getting tougher every morning to get up and see smoke curling out of the chimney of Amber's warm, snug cabin. This trip was beginning to slowly wear us down. It wasn't hard hunting, it was just hard to be living out there. We weren't looking for the Ritz when we came to Alaska, but it was no pleasure to get up each morning and head afield when everything you owned was frozen stiffer than five dollars' worth of jawbreakers.

Finally one morning Terry flew in with his old black plane to check on us. When he determined we were fine but didn't have any moose, he suggested we work farther up the valley, where more moose traditionally congregated at that time of the year. Since we weren't seeing a whole lot around base camp, we decided to do just that. The problem was, the area we wanted to hunt was too far to reach in a single day's ride out and back, so we made the decision to pack some light supplies and the pup tents and strike out, rough-camping it out there until we found moose.

We rode north of the spike camp into the valley for an entire day until we started seeing moose sign. When we stopped for the night, moose sign was prevalent all around us, and as we were pitching the tents we heard a bull grunt off in the timber. Finally we were among them!

The next morning we awoke full of anticipation. We quickly reheated some Hamburger Helper and wolfed that down before heading out. We were just 200, maybe 300 yards from camp when we completely sunk one of the horses to his neck in an icy bog. It was easy to see that this horse was gonna die if we didn't do something.

He was stuck in half-frozen mud and water and he just plain gave up.

We worked for over an hour pulling, pushing, and hitting him with small branches, trying to get him to move. We finally got him out of the bog, but it was just so frustrating—to travel all the way to Alaska, then to fly in to a remote cabin, ride a full day to our spike camp, then ride another full day to fly camp, and still not really get to hunt because of rugged Alaskan conditions.

But our luck was about to change. It wasn't long after getting the horse unstuck that we walked up over a ridge and heard a moose grunt. We started looking for him and sure enough out walked a decent bull. He was right around the 50-inch mark. He strolled out of the timber and literally right by me at 15 yards. Since we were not exactly sure how wide he was (Alaska law in this area required a 50-inch outside antler spread minimum) I let him keep walking. In hindsight we realized he was legal, but we sure as heck didn't want to make a mistake.

Before long we heard another bull grunt down across the valley. Because of where he was, Rhett and I split up, hoping one of us would get a shot with a bow. When I got settled in, I set up a Montana moose decoy and we started calling. It wasn't long before I spotted that bull 300 yards away, coming down the far hillside. It was a magnificent sight, he was big and black, with antlers as large as bow cases on either side. He was plowing through knee-deep snow on a line right to us. He finally got to 30 yards but didn't stop or turn—he was heading right at us, which is no great angle for a shot with a bow. All of the sudden, at about 25 yards out, he cut to the side to go around a big wall of brush and stopped, looking right at us. I really didn't have a good shot as he was standing behind some brush, but I knew it was now or never and I had to make the shot. So I drew back and looked for a hole I could shoot through. I found a spot I thought I could get an arrow through and let one fly at this wall of hide, muscle, and bone that looked as big as a barn.

Well the hole proved true and the 115-grain Muzzy just smoked him in the boiler room. The bull spun around and took off toward Rhett. From Rhett's vantage point, he couldn't tell that I had shot, he just knew that the bull was crashing toward him and figured that the bull had just committed to his calling and was coming, so he got ready and the cameraman started rolling tape. When the bull got 150 yards away from Rhett, he hit a brush patch and just stopped. Within a few seconds, Rhett and the cameraman heard him crash to the ground,

Grinning, Rhett exclaimed, "Gol-dangit! Waddell just done and killed our bull."

When I walked up to the bull, Rhett was already there waiting for me with a grin on his face. It was a cool experience.

After we got the bull, I came to find out that this was only the second bull Pioneer Outfitters had got with a bow, and it was Brian's first guiding experience with a bowhunter. He later confessed to me that he had doubted a bow's effectiveness on moose, but now that he saw the results of a well-placed arrow he was fired up for it.

Now the work began. This was my first moose and I couldn't believe how big he was, lying there on the ground. So now the moose hunt was pretty much over for everyone until we got this bull dressed, quartered up, and packed out. We started working and before we realized it, it was one in the morning.

So we called it quits for the day and returned the following morning with the horses to pack out all the meat. Instead of just bringing the meat to our fly camp, we decided to haul it all the way back to the spike camp. We rode pretty much all day and into the night before we got back, and we were some kind of wore out when we finally unsaddled the horses.

The following day was a complete washout for Rhett as far as any hunting was concerned, as we had to cape out the head and prepare all the meat for transport out of the spike camp and back to Terry's lodge.

We were now into this hunt eight days and Rhett really hadn't had a chance to unleash an arrow. We had one more day to hunt before Terry was scheduled to come back and get us. Since Rhett had the concert at the Air Force base, the plan was for Terry to come get us out with his plane, while the guides broke down camp for the season and packed all the gear out on horses.

The evening before the final day of hunting we decided the only chance for Rhett to get a bull was to return back to the country where I got mine. So we saddled up the horses once again and started riding. This time we went even further than where I shot my bull, and we threw up another fly camp for the short night's rest.

The next morning we got up and headed up a big draw. We hadn't climbed far when we started seeing cow moose all over the side of the mountain quite a way off. Before we could decide what to do, we looked back to our right and there was just a P-I-G of a bull, about 200 yards away from us, walking toward those cows. Well, Rhett had brought along a T/C Encore in .300 Win. Mag. just in case, and since this was the last day of the hunt, he decided it was time to use the long-range bow. The guide said, "Oh my . . . that is definitely a Boone and Crockett bull, you need to kill him."

So Rhett got all settled in with the rifle and squeezed off a shot. Now, a moose is as big as a barn, but he didn't pull a hair. The bull jumped at the shot, but just kept walking toward the cows. In all, Rhett took four or five shots, all with similar results. For his part, the bull never broke stride, he just kept heading for the cows. Rhett was deflated. "I was on him every shot. I don't know if the rifle is off or I jerked the trigger or what." The guides were equally frustrated. Here was a chance to end the hunt on a high note and it wasn't coming together. One of the guides said, "Well, that was a good chance. Let's head back to camp."

I replied, "No way. We have four hours left before dark, we are going to keep hunting."

I figured we might still have a crack at this bull. He had dropped over a small ridge, but we never saw him come up the other side, so we took off running toward where he went over. Now, it didn't look all that far, but in big country like Alaska, the distance is deceiving—it turned out to be a long ways. It took us two hours before we finally got to the spot where the bull had crossed over the ridge. It was now about an hour before sunset, but the sun was already starting to dip behind the high mountains. We snuck up and peered over the ridge and lo and behold there was that bull, with two cows, standing there, looking back up the ridge at us.

We both knew it was now or never, so Rhett got down, laid out his pack to get a steady rifle rest. I spoke to him quietly, "Rhett, just take your time and squeeze." He did and when the report echoed back from the far mountains, we knew it was all over but the crying. He had just poleaxed the bull. Never moving a muscle, that grand monarch of the North simply tipped over right there.

Well, we were so pumped we just came unglued, whooping and hollering and jumping all around the place. All of us were just emotionally and physically beat, but now we had a lot of work ahead of us. It was getting dark quickly. We had a big bull down that we had to deal with, plus we still had a five-hour ride back to spike camp, where Terry was going to pick us up the following morning. We quartered up the bull, but the thought of packing him up on the horses and riding for five hours was just too much to stand.

We were all so cold and worn out we just didn't care. We needed a break. So we moved away from the bull a bit, in case of bears, and pitched our two little tents. We then built a fire big enough they could see it back in Alabama. We were so exhausted that when we crawled into those little tents on the side of some snow-covered mountain in Alaska, they were as comfortable as a bed at the Hilton.

. . .

We slept like the dead that night, the wind howling around the outside of our little compound. At dawn the next morning we woke up, revived and rested, but knew we now had to hump. The plane was coming that day and we still had that long ride back to the spike camp. So Rhett and I broke camp while the guides hurriedly put the quarters on the pack horses. No longer was there a distinction between guides and clients, at this point everyone was equal. We all had jobs to do to get out of the wilderness, and we all pitched in with equal effort.

We got everything loaded up and we saddled up and took off. After a five-hour ride, we finally arrived back in camp, fully expecting Terry to be there waiting for us, probably ticked that he had to wait, but there was no sign of him. It was kind of foggy out and we guessed that he couldn't make it in. Rhett had a concert to get to and I had a commercial flight out of Anchorage a day and a half later, but there was nothing to be done about it. We kept our bags packed, ready to go at first light, and turned in for a fitful night's sleep.

The next day we had breakfast, caped out Rhett's moose head, cleaned up around camp, and generally just waited. We were reluctant to tear down the wall tent in case Terry didn't come, which turned out to be a good decision as he didn't make it in that day, either. Now I knew I wasn't going to make my commercial flight, as it was the following morning and we were still in the middle of the Wrangell Mountains. To top that off, Rhett was supposed to be giving a concert that night at the Air Force base, which obviously wasn't going to happen, either. We had no satellite phone and no way to communicate with the Air Force folks to let them know Rhett was not going to be able to make the concert.

We had now been in the bush twelve days and really started to panic, not because we were worried about surviving or anything like that, as we had shelter, food, and water, but because we had commitments that we couldn't make and no way to let people know. I was sure my wife would be freaking out when I didn't arrive home as scheduled. I knew work would probably be wondering what happened. Rhett had fans waiting to hear some music at the show he didn't appear for, and to top it all off, I only had three days at home before I was scheduled to turn around and head out again for another TV show. We all had commitments that we needed to take care of, but this was Alaska and we were stuck.

But, as the old saying goes, no use crying over spilt milk. There was really nothing Rhett, the guides, myself, or Terry could do about it. If the weather is bad in Alaska, you have to wait it out—that is all you can do. So we tried to entertain ourselves and keep busy. We kept cleaning up around camp, every so often we would shovel off the runway so Terry could land, and we did a lot of sitting around the fire, playing the guitar.

After three or four days of this, we finally heard a plane coming. So we all went running out to the runway, excited to see Terry. But he just flew over low, opened the window, and yelled. We made out his words, but just barely . . .

The words "I can't get you" were drawn out across the wind and snow and felt just as lonely as they sounded. With that, the black plane banked away and headed back for Terry's main camp.

Well, this event didn't make us feel any better at all. We were all getting a mite frustrated now. The weather was miserable and it was getting colder by the day as we were getting well into October. I walked into our wall tent that night feeling pretty low. Steve and Rhett were already in their sleeping bags, fully dressed of course, and still shivering. I looked at them and I had had enough. I had spent fifteen days in the same clothes, since it was too cold while camping to take your heavy hunting gear off. I could smell myself and I hadn't had a decent night's sleep in nearly two weeks. So I grabbed my sleeping bag and pillow and headed for the cabin. When I entered, Amber was sitting there in cutoff sweatpants and a T-shirt, 'cause it was nice and warm in there next to the woodstove. I didn't say a word, just threw my bag down on the floor under the kitchen table and started preparing for my first good night's sleep of the whole trip.

Before I could get settled, she said, "What are you doing? You can't sleep in here!"

"No . . . I *am* gonna sleep in here. This is bullshit. You can cut my throat in the middle of the night if you want to, but I am not sleeping another night in that freezing wall tent. My butt is sleeping in the place where the fire is. I ain't that dumb. It's the warmest place in camp, which obviously you know as you have been sleeping here the whole damn time."

She protested a bit more, but I just ignored her. I climbed into my sleeping bag and went to sleep.

The next morning, Rhett and Steve came in and looked at me. Immediately Rhett said, "That was the last night I sleep in a wall tent too."

The guides and Steve quickly chimed in.

"You all can't sleep in here," Amber protested.

"Yes we can!" was the unified response. That night everyone slept in the cabin, guides and all.

Luckily the next day Terry managed to land and explained that he had been trying to come get us for several days but each day the weather was either bad at our camp or at his main cabin. Now there was a break in the weather, so we quickly loaded our personal belongings, piled into the plane, and got transported the thirty or so miles to Terry's base camp. The moment we landed he said, "Hurry up and grab the rest of your gear and we'll take off for town." By the time we got back out to the plane with our hard bow cases and the luggage we'd left at the main camp, Terry said, "Too late. The window closed."

We spent another two days with Terry at the main camp, which at least had power, communication with the outside world, a VCR (I think I watched *Sling Blade* 133 times), and a warm shower. All this taught me a very valuable lesson: Sometimes when things are out of your control, you gotta just go with the flow. Alaskan residents have mastered this art. If the weather is bad, and they can't fly, they don't risk it. It is simply foolish. They sit down, brew some coffee, and relax, spending the day talking, reminiscing about past hunts, and just enjoying life. It is a lifestyle that, once accustomed to, makes a lot of sense.

This aspect of detachment from the outside world really didn't fully sink in with me until some months after the hunt. When we first arrived at camp, we had to buy our hunting licenses and tags from Terry. The bill came to $2,500 or so for both Rhett and me, as we got hunting licenses, bear tags, wolf tags, and moose tags. Now, I don't make it a habit to carry much cash on me, a little bit to tip guides and buy some meals, but not much. If someone ever knocks me over the head for my wallet they will be mightily disappointed. So, at any rate, I handed Terry my credit card, to which he responded, "No, we just take cash or checks."

Well, I didn't have either, so I said, "Well, I am good for it." Terry accepted that and essentially let me give him an IOU. I seriously hate owing anybody any money, so I made it my first priority when I got home to write Terry a check. I literally walked in the door, kissed my wife, then grabbed the checkbook. I put the check in the mail and left again on a hunting trip.

December rolled around and I finally got a break in my schedule. I was going over some past bills and looking at my checking balance and I noticed my check to Terry never cleared the bank. Fearing it got lost in the mail, and embarrassed as I didn't want Terry thinking I stiffed him, I called him immediately.

"Hey, Terry, this is Michael Waddell. I just noticed that check I sent you never cleared my account, did you get it?"

"No, I don't think I got it. I remember that you were going to send me a check, but I don't remember ever seeing it. Let me look through my stuff and see if it is here somewhere and I'll call you back."

When he called me back he said, "No, we don't have it. But I'll tell ya what I'm going to do—I haven't checked the mail in a little while, so let me run down to the mailbox on the snow machine to make sure it isn't there and I'll call ya back."

Well, I figured that check should have arrived long ago and was now as good as lost. When he said he hadn't checked the mailbox in a little while, I assumed he meant in the last few days and he was just going through a good-faith effort to make sure it wasn't there, stuck to the side or something.

A little while later my phone rang and it was Terry.

"Yup, got yer check."

"Terry, I can't believe it took so long to get up there. What does the postmark say?"

"It says October."

"Terry, is this the first time you have been to the mailbox since October?"

"Uh, yeah, yeah, we have been kind of busy wrapping everything up."

So for two months, they had little to no contact with the outside world. That blew me away. I have been to some slow-moving places in my life, but none as slow as rural Alaska. I found it very refreshing and a good life lesson. Even in our hectic life in the Lower 48, it would do us all some good to turn off the TV once in a while, shut off the cell phone, and just enjoy the simpler things.

12

BWANA WADDELL

U nlike Alaska, Africa was not a childhood dream
for me. But as I grew older, that dream developed,
and the more I started being successful with a bow
and arrow, the more the Dark Continent began to call
to me.

What I really thought I knew about Africa—at least
from what I'd read and seen on TV—was that it was a
T-A-R-G-E-T R-I-C-H environment. To be truly and
completely honest, I love to kill. Yes, I am a hunter, and
I hunt to kill. The bonuses I get out of it are the wonders of wildlife, the experience, and the culture. Most
people usually have a 180-degree different response to
the question "Why do you hunt?" Most say it is for the
experience. I say it is for the kill. Most claim they hunt
to experience the wonders of wildlife and that the kill

is a bonus. Either I am just different or maybe more honest about myself. To me it is the kill that makes hunting real, and makes one appreciate the natural world so acutely. To those who just watch wildlife, I say: You are missing out and are more of a spectator than a participant in the natural cycle.

Does that mean the kill is the only thing that is important? No, absolutely not. You see things firsthand when hunting, often while miserable, that you would see in no other time or place. I absolutely hate to sit all day long in freezing weather, but I do it to be successful. Yet even when I am not successful, hardly a day goes by that I don't see something I would not have seen if I'd stayed at home. It might be a doe pawing at another doe, or an immature buck trying to fight, or simply a sunrise through frosty tree limbs. The point is, there is a lot to appreciate and be thankful for when sitting in the woods. But if we weren't looking to fill a tag, most of us would never get the chance to experience this.

The sheer amount of stuff to kill is what really drew me to Africa. In addition to the abundance of targets, another draw is the climate. Having grown up in the South, I like warm weather. Last time I checked, Africa makes the grade for warmth. Add in the large amount of game, the many opportunities to kill, the warm environment and unique culture, and you have a ready-made place to dull a quiver full of broadheads.

When first-timers think of plains-game hunting in Africa, almost everyone wants a big kudu and a gemsbok, and I was no different. But I was also intrigued to see what else was there. If you just go to Africa looking for a trophy kudu you may spend all week waiting for just that one opportunity, and it might not come. But if you are open-minded and willing to shoot at impala, blesbok, warthog, duiker, or one of the dozens of other species whose names I can't even pronounce—and which even a wildlife biologist would have a hard time with—then you will be thoroughly entertained by sitting over a water hole, watching the red African sun plunge toward the desert floor and listening for the pitter-patter of hoofed feet.

So with all this in mind, I decided it was time to go to Africa. I was twenty-nine years old. I had hunted tons of states and a few remote places in Canada and Mexico and now I wanted to see what the Dark Continent was really like. I boarded a plane in Atlanta with little true knowledge of what to expect. This is possibly the only negative aspect of going to Africa— the long flight. You get on the plane, eat, watch a movie or two, eat again, sleep for a while, wake up, eat again, watch another movie, and then you realize you still have another ten hours to go! Unless you have flown around the world, you can't imagine the boredom of it. After eighteen hours in the air, from Atlanta nonstop across the Atlantic Ocean, we arrived in Johannesburg, South Africa. While Johannesburg is a big city, it just feels like Africa. Natives, skyscrapers, and Land Rovers all combine to let you know you are no longer in Atlanta. From Johannesburg, we got on a smaller plane bound for the tiny town of Polokawane in the northern province in South Africa, from which we drove a couple hours into the country, or veld, as it is called there, arriving finally at Ken Moody's camp. Like almost all in South Africa, this hunting area is private and high-fenced. But unlike many high-fenced areas in the United States, the amount of property managed is simply staggering. Ranches of 10,000 acres are common, and ranches sprawling over 100,000 acres are not that far out of the norm. The fencing in South Africa is not so much about artificially managing or enhancing wildlife as it is about protecting it from native poaching. It just goes to show ya that rednecks are rednecks, regardless of their skin color. If the property wasn't fenced, you can bet that some ole local natives would be slippin' up there at night and whacking the bejesus out of the game . . . which really is not too different from Georgia!

High-fence hunting has been a hot topic in the hunting world and probably became more so with the popularity of outdoor television shows, where some folks hunt almost exclusively within an enclosure. Like I said about ethics versus laws, I really don't have a problem with someone who wants to hunt behind a fence, provided it is legal in that state. Now, I have seen some places in the South, especially in Texas, where I would be pretty hard-pressed to call what they do "hunting." It is more like killing, but without the element of sport. I would never have a desire to go "hunting" there, 'cause that's not hunting at all.

Well, if all of a sudden I wanted to taste some backstraps and a guy said I could shoot that 170-inch deer within the fence, I ain't saying I wouldn't kill it. But I sure as heck wouldn't call it hunting. And I sure as hell wouldn't be figuring out a way to get that deer on the next grunt call box or try to tell people that I am the best rattler or grunter, or I found a new snort wheeze that makes deer come running in doing backflips because of this 170-inch deer. I didn't hunt him, I just killed him. But in Africa, the high fences were surrounding such ginormous territory, it sure as hell *was* hunting.

That first day we just relaxed, unpacked gear, shot our bows, and tried to get over the jet lag. We met with our PH (professional hunter), Niko Neuhoff, and went over photos of the various animals found in the region. Niko tried to explain the differences between a good trophy and an average trophy, as well as the correct shot placement for the various African species. Interestingly enough, the vitals in African game for the most part sit much lower and further forward than in most North American game.

The next day found myself and Mark Womack overlooking our first African water hole from the comfort of a sunken ground blind. While I don't really enjoy ground blind water-hole hunting in North America, in Africa it is different, mainly because of the amount of game present. We weren't in the blind more than half an hour when I caught movement coming through the sparse African scrub. Presently, a small brown antelope emerged and tentatively started for the water hole. From my brief education with Niko and his photo book, it was obvious this antelope was a duiker or a steinbok. To tell the truth, I wasn't really sure, but I did know one thing—it wasn't a kudu. All I knew was that both steinboks and duikers were okay to shoot, and both were included in my package, and he was standing broadside at 25 yards. I mentally decided it was a duiker and drew back. I concentrated hard on the front pin, as they aren't a big target, only having a four-to-five-inch vital area, and squeezed the trigger. The arrow smacked the duiker and he dropped on the spot. After checking out the four-inch horns, I picked up the radio and called Ken Moody.

"Duiker down. Duiker down. Bring the big truck, we may need to winch."

When Niko and Ken arrived on the scene, they took one look at it and Niko said, "Nice steinbok."

"That's what I said—*steinbok*. The radio must not have been working right."

Since the day was still early, Ken and Niko left Mark and me in the blind with instructions to wait out the rest of the day, since it was likely more animals would come in. After an hour or so, a group of female impalas came in, along with a small kudu bull and cow. After that, a small group of warthogs came in and watered. I passed up all the animals and just enjoyed watching the show; it was like having a front-row seat in a National Geographic documentary. It was getting on to late afternoon, nearly early evening, when I first saw black movement coming through the brush. At first I wasn't sure what it was, but then I saw the stripes and knew it was one of Africa's most common antelope species, the blue wildebeest. As he moved closer, it was obvious that he was a solitary old bull, well into his prime, and from the little I knew of African species, a great-looking trophy. For those who think African animals are easy, this bull was as wary as anything I have ever hunted. He slowly worked his way in, circling the water hole, checking for scent. He finally got within 25 yards, facing broadside, when I came to full draw and released an arrow. The Beman shaft sunk to the fletching right behind the shoulder, angling into the vitals. The bull took off in a mad kicking dash but didn't go far before dying. I watched him drop within sight of the blind. I was ecstatic. While the steinbok was a unique African trophy, and my first, this bull was something to behold. As I walked up to him, I was shocked at how wonderfully striped the hide was, and the horns were polished black, with blunt, heavy tips. He surely was an old bull. Niko and Ken came with the truck and this time they did need the winch.

Words cannot describe Africa even though volumes have been written on it and countless TV shows have tried to bring it into your living room. Nothing can truly prepare you for what this primitive place does to the spirit and soul of a hunter. I think it affects hunters differently than tourists, photographers, or missionaries. There is a spirit in the air that is there all the time, and it was different from what I have experienced anywhere in North America. Even though South Africa looked a lot like Texas, it sure didn't feel like Texas. I fell in love with that feel even more than I did with the hunting.

I have always had a severe case of ADD. If things aren't happening, I get bored and want to make my own luck. This is often the case with experienced hunters, more so than with novices. It seems like sometimes the more experience you get in the field, the more your mind races ahead, always coming up with a plan B or C if plan A doesn't immediately bear fruit. But in Africa my ADD was absent. I was never bored; I was always entertained at the sights, sounds, and smells at a water hole. There is an intensity there, a feeling that something is about to happen, or something just did happen just out of range of your ears and eyes. It is spiritual and palpable. It put something in my soul that intrigued me.

Africa is often erroneously labeled in our industry and in our hunting society as a high-end, hoity-toity endeavor, but I am still as redneck as they come and I loved it. I enjoy simple hunts. I still enjoy floating jugs for catfish, gigging for bullfrogs, catching crappies, or shooting a limit of squirrels to fry up. That all being said, I really enjoyed Africa and found it to be pretty daggum down-to-earth. If you have a hunting spirit in you, Africa has a way of putting it in overdrive. Rich, poor, or middle-class, you will feel at home on safari if you are truly a hunter.

Most people never let themselves dream about Africa or let themselves think they would enjoy it. But if they do, I am the first to warn ya, it is opening a valve that cannot easily be closed. If it gets a hold on ya, it is a serious passion.

Over the course of several days I shot an eland, a wildebeest, two impala, and a steinbok. I could have killed other animals, as pretty much anything is legal if it comes in to the water hole. I just had to keep in mind what I could afford, as everything carries an individual price.

My time in Africa came to an end before it really ever began. Someone wrote long ago that your soul takes a while to catch up with your physical body when you are traveling, and I think that is what happened to me. Just when I started to feel at home in Africa, and when my soul had reunited with my body, I had to physically get back on a plane, and left my soul wandering around the African continent, asking random natives if they had seen a soulless-looking redneck from Booger Bottom anywhere. I am also told once you drink the waters of Africa, you will return again to quench your thirst.

Either I needed to find my soul or just get a drink, but I knew one thing for sure. I had to go back to the place where lions roar.

AFRICA REVISITED

My second trip to Africa was completely different from my first. I had done some research and discovered a little place where the lions still roared, where tribal traditions still survive, and where to some of the predators, people were just as tasty as impalas. That little place is Botswana. Of course if you ever look at a map of Africa, you will quickly realize that Botswana is far from little. It is roughly the size of Montana and Wyoming put together. It is home to the Okavango Delta, which is the world's largest inland delta, where millions of gallons of water run into the desert and simply disappear into the African sands. The country is inhabited mainly by the Tswana tribe, but there are also quite a few poison-arrow-shooting aboriginal bushmen living there in case it starts feeling too civilized. Considering there are only a few roads and only a couple major airports in the whole bloody place, you realize pretty quickly that Botswana brings a new meaning to the word "remote."

On this trip, we were filming for my new show *Bone Collector* and we were after dangerous game: buffalo and elephant. I was to hunt the buffalo, and Aaron Neilson of Global Hunting Resources was going to shoot an elephant. I have always thought Cape buffalo were cool and had dreamed of hunting them. As a professional hunter once said to me, "Cape buffalo are a lot like lawyers: they are mean and ugly and you really are doing the world a favor by getting rid of a few of them." While killing one by any means would be exciting, I really wanted to hunt one with a bow, like Fred Bear did in Mozambique with Wally Johnson so many years before. So I worked with my bow, cranked it all the way up, and sighted in heavier arrows. Alas, the year before I went, the Botswana game department decided to outlaw hunting dangerous game with a bow. However, I decided to do the next best thing and take a T/C muzzleloader to add some extra excitement to the hunt.

Landing in Victoria Falls, Zimbabwe, is quite a shock for those who have never been there before. Zimbabwe is one of the wealthiest countries in all of Africa in terms of natural resources, but it has been thrust into abject poverty by Robert Mugabe, the country's president/dictator. This destitution is apparent as soon as you land at the airport. The airport must have been nice once, as it was originally set up for tourists, but now it is a wreck. To put it into perspective, Victoria Falls is one of the seven natural wonders of the world, yet there is no merchandise in any of the airport shops, and the furniture is missing—having been stolen—from the restaurants and bars. If you venture into any of the cities, you will see the same. No products in the stores, no food on the shelves, no gas at the gas stations, and most cities suffer from frequent electrical black-outs. Mugabe's revolution for native freedom has done little to improve the living conditions of the citizens. It is really a shame, for the country is simply magnificent in scenery, and the common people are very friendly.

I met up with Nick Mundt, Steve Finch, and Aaron Neilson and headed for the Ultimate Lodge—that really is the name of it. The lodge caters only to hunters. If you are a sightseer, tourist, photographer, or nature watcher you can't stay there—my kind of place! Only those with bullets or arrows are allowed.

The next morning we all got up, excited to do some stuff like take a helicopter flight around the falls, and possibly some bungee jumping over the Zambezi River. Well, I dug into my bag to retrieve some cash—I had brought US$4,500 with me for any-thing I might need, sightseeing, presents for the kids, or bribe money to get back home, etc.—and it was all gone. To this day, I don't know where it went, I imagine it was one of the fifty porters who rushed to "help" me in the Jo'burg airport, but it really didn't matter how it disappeared. I was now in Zimbabwe, flat broke, with twenty-two more days to stay in Africa. I have been short of cash before, but you don't really know what honest-to-goodness broke feels like until you end up busted in a Third World country. The nearest ATM was probably a thousand miles away. There was no way of wiring money, no such thing as a checkbook, and no using your credit card to withdraw money . . . I'm talkin' serious *broke*! I have never felt so financially naked in my life. Luckily my buddies floated me a loan until I was stateside. I don't know what I would have done without them.

To make matters worse, at that time in Zimbabwe, "democratic" elections were being held, and Mugabe had pretty much shut down everything in the country to stop information from getting around. Cell phones didn't work, nor did land lines, and you could forget about using credit cards or accessing the Internet—the country had ground to a stop.

We decided to make the best of it and went on a helicopter ride around the falls. If you ever get to Africa, and make it all the way to Victoria Falls, this is one thing you should do. It is simply amazing. After our sophisticated, *National Geographic*–style heli tour, we reverted back to our redneck selves and grabbed fishin' poles, but instead of catfish we went looking for the infamous tiger fish. Not misnamed in the slightest, these toothsome monsters inhabit the Zambezi River and Lake Kariba (as well as many other bodies of water in Africa) and get pretty darn huge. Considering that we were going after a fish with a mouth full of razor blades, in full view of the Nile crocs sunning themselves in the shallows, it made sense to me why you don't see a lot of party boats with water slides on Lake Kariba.

The tiger fish were incredible. Think of a saltwater fish mixed with a northern pike and you can start to imagine what they are like. In spite of my money getting stolen and various other travel hassles, we all started to realize that maybe Africa ain't too bad a place after all. Now we were ready to continue our journey into Botswana, where animals with black horns and ivory tusks awaited us.

We finally made it to the Botswana camp, where we would be hunting with Ronnie Blackbeard. The Blackbeard family is legendary in Africa. A long line of professional hunters, they definitely represent the culture of hunting in Africa.

Right off the bat we went out hunting, and it was just amazing country. Since I was hunting buffalo and Aaron was hunting elephant, we hunted together.

The plan was, if we cut buff tracks we would go after them and I would kill a buff; if we found big elephant tracks, we would track them down and Aaron would shoot one if a good bull was found.

It was a shock for me to see the number of elephants that live in Botswana. It is simply amazing. In America, many have the impression that elephants are endangered and rare, but that is really not the case. We were seeing hundreds of elephants every day, and it was easy to see they were more than the carrying capacity of the land. The country looked like one big clear-cut, with no mature trees, and the reason for this is that the vast herds of elephants have simply pushed them all over for food.

While we were seeing lots of elephants, most were cows and calves and some smaller bulls. Aaron was looking for a bull that would have ivory of at least fifty pounds per side—in other words, a "good bull." To be honest, I wouldn't have known a fifty-pounder from Dumbo, as they all looked big to me.

It's funny how hunting culture differs from place to place. We see this in America, where guys in Texas don't hunt like the guys in Michigan and there is a little rivalry between the various sects of hunting technique; but one thing that is universally disdained in America is road hunting, or using vehicles to find game. This is not the case in Africa. I thought I had ridden lots in the back of trucks, growing up in Georgia, but not compared to Africa. We spent a week riding around in the back of Land Rovers, looking for elephant tracks. To the uninitiated this may not seem that sporting, but after looking over miles and miles of African real estate, I see why they do it. You have to cover lots of miles to find a good bull, and when you do find a good bull track, you will still have miles of walking before you catch up with him.

On the third or fourth day, we cut some really fresh buffalo track, probably less than three hours old, judging from the dung, so we decided to go after them. Merikee the tracker got on the spoor and we followed at top speed. After about an hour and a half of tracking we got into the herd. As we got closer we started picking out black shadows in the dense green bush and it wasn't long before we ended up slipping right up on an old bull. He looked good to me but he didn't impress Ronnie, so we passed him, even though we were only 30 yards away. One bit of advice I have found true about Africa is: trust your guide. When your PH becomes excited, you should, too; but if they are not excited about an animal, it is for good reason. So we kept easing up through there and quickly realized we were on the fringes of a pretty good-sized herd. Well, about the time we begin looking at some more bulls, the wind shifts and alerts them. In no time they blow and stampede out of there. But they didn't completely leave the country, so we kept tracking them and got back on the herd within another hour or so. But the wind proved fickle again and they blew out of there once more. After repeating this process for three hours, we circled way around and got back into them with the right wind. We snuck back up through there and immediately spotted several nice bulls, but then a monster bull stepped out. He was just a giant, noticeably larger both in body and horn than the other good bulls around him. As soon as he stepped clear of the other bulls he spotted us and turned toward us, quartering pretty hard to us, looking right at us. Since he was only 35 yards or so away, I decided to take the shot. I felt the muzzleloader would be up for the task of breaking the front leg and penetrating into the vitals as I had it stoked up with a 450-grain jacketed bullet backed by 150 grains of Pyrodex.

I put the sights in line with his leg, a third of the way up his body, and pulled the trigger. When the smoke cleared and I watched the bull run off, I knew I had made the biggest mistake of my African hunting career. I knew I hit him exactly where I was aiming, and when we reviewed the tapes it was confirmed I hit him perfectly, but when we went to look for spoor, there was hardly any blood. The little blood we were finding was low on the brush and looked like it was dripping out and running down his leg, not the spray that is so typical of a vital-shot animal. We all knew I didn't get enough penetration.

We kept tracking him, and eventually caught up to him, but as soon as we got sight of him, he took off running. This disheartened me more than anything because I could tell he wasn't mortally hit. According to experienced buff hunters, if you come up on a mortally wounded bull he will charge or at least hold his ground, but for a bull to run off with the rest of the herd is a pretty good indication he is not mortally wounded. As soon as he got back into the herd, while we continued to track them for while, it became evident that we were not going to be able to find him again. The dust stopped the bleeding, and with all the other tracks, it was impossible to sort him out. So my buffalo hunting career was rather short-lived. I was devastated, and more than a little mad at myself. Losing this buff really wasn't equipment failure but knowledge failure on how to use the equipment on my part. I should have known better than to take a shot that was suitable for a rifle with a muzzleloader. Had I waited and got a broadside shot or a quartering-away shot I am convinced the T/C would have done its part, but a quartering-to shot on a large buff is just more than a muzzleloader bullet can handle.

To add insult to injury, since I drew blood my hunt was over. So I traveled halfway around the world, spent a considerable amount of money, and all I left with was an education and a passion to return someday to try again. But for the time being I would spend the next eighteen days in Africa as a cheerleader for everyone else, which while not as good as hunting yourself, still beats working for a living.

Our camp situated in the Chobe region was simply magnificent. Comprised of traditional wall tents with luxury furnishings, it was the kind of camp Teddy Roosevelt may have stayed in on his safari. Every night we would sit by the campfire, then go to sleep with the sounds of hyenas and lions in the background. In that cool desert air, without a cell phone, I have never slept more soundly.

I decided to maximize the hunting experience by tagging along with Aaron in his quest for an old bull elephant. Every morning we would either spot an elephant or find bull tracks and then take off for hours on end stalking bulls. But every time we finally got close enough to look one over carefully, it was a bull we didn't want to shoot. This type of hunting is vastly different from what I was used to. It wasn't about being stealthy, it was about covering lots of terrain in search of the right animal. Once found it was relatively straightforward to walk in and get a shot. Still, just being out there was an education in itself. Along the way, we saw several cool things. Lion tracks abound and often we would cut tracks of big male lions in the sand and once even spooked one off a kill. We cut leopard tracks and witnessed where one had made a kill and dragged the animal up into a tree to feed. It is this kind of stuff that makes Africa so special. You may be going after one species, but around you there is the life-and-death struggle of predator and prey constantly. The food chain is alive and well in Africa.

Finally, after eight days of this, we cut the track of an old bull. He was running with two juvenile bulls. Evidently, according to Ronnie Blackbeard, old bulls like this will run with younger bulls who have better senses for protection, and it has clearly been displayed time and time again across Africa that these younger bulls will protect the old bull. Well, as it turned out, these juvenile bulls weren't very good at their job, and we snuck right in on him. He turned and flapped his ears and we got a good look at his ivory. He was at least a fifty-pounder. While he was looking right at us, we crouched and snuck in a little closer and got to around

45 yards when he flapped his ears and started to come. It wasn't a full-blown charge, but he was coming to check us out and run us out of there if he could. Aaron pulled up his .375 H&H loaded with Barnes monolithic solids and made one heck of a frontal brain shot, dumping him on the spot.

Walking up to him, it was one of the wildest experiences of my life. Seeing your first dead elephant on the ground is something that almost defies description. They are just simply huge. I could barely pick up the front section of his trunk, he was so large. We sat there and simply gawked. Ronnie cut off the tail and gave it to Aaron, which is the traditional symbolic right of ownership.

The trackers went back to camp to round up some more help for the butchering job. When they returned they had a slew of people, I think the whole village turned out to get some meat. They brought a tractor into the bush, towing a large trailer. One piece at a time, we cut up that bull, taking every bit of meat, and when we were done, the trailer was overflowing. The next day the meat was to be delivered to a local village. Curious as to how the process worked, I decided to tag along.

Evidently there are four villages within the hunting concession and they are on a rotation schedule for donation of elephant meat. Now, what I saw really didn't set too well with me. To begin with, we were there paying huge money for the chance to hunt elephant; the meat is an added bonus the natives get from the hunt, but do you think they would have sent a tractor out to get the meat? The tractor and trailer we used to donate the meat to these villagers had to be rented from them, and we had to pay for it. The theory that God helps those that help themselves is obviously not too well known in these parts.

Since the village in question was the farthest from where we killed the bull, we had to go through all the other villages before we got to the one we were donating the meat to. As you can imagine, by the time we got to the village, a large part of the meat had been swiped off the back of the trailer by natives from the other villages. So much for sharing with your fellow tribesmen in an organized way. When we arrived, everyone in the village turned out, dads, granddads, moms, daughters, sons, babies, and every dog in the village, and they all wanted a scrap of meat. They were aggravated over the loss of some of their meat. The first words the tribal leader said to me when we pulled up were: "You didn't bring enough meat."

All I could think to say was, "Well, it's an elephant, it was the biggest damn thing we could find. Outside of harpooning a whale, it was as good as we could do."

Immediately he was offended that there wasn't more meat, even though there was more than enough to go around for everyone in his village, and I was offended that he was being so greedy and unappreciative of what we were doing for him. Hunting was the number-one resource in that area, but they were so dependent upon hunters that it was not only pathetic but sickening. Every nice building in that village, every maize grinder, every well, and every funeral facility was bought by hunters' money, and on top of that they were being fed at our expense. I felt good about us being hunters and providers and giving something back, but at the same time when I realized how dependent and apathetic these people were, I really didn't feel that good.

The natives I saw—not all of them, mind you, but a large percentage—consider themselves victims. In my humble Georgia opinion, the reason they are victims is because they wake up victims every day. Every morning when they get up, they are waiting for somebody, whether it is the government, social workers, or people like me, to give them something or help them in some way. Independence is crucial for a society, as well as for an individual, to be successful. If you are dependent on your government or anyone else to provide for you, there is no motivation to take care of yourself and prosper.

. . .

What I saw in Africa showed me that welfare doesn't work, that governments outside of true democracies quickly become horribly corrupt, and that in the end both things hurt the populace. While I didn't leave Africa with a load of trophy animals, I did leave with a rejuvenated appreciation for America. No matter how bad our economy gets, in America we have a lot to be thankful for. We have freedom, our prosperity, and material possessions only dreamed about in the rest of the world. We didn't get this by being lucky, we got this through hard work and independence, and I don't care who you are or how "disadvantaged" you think you are, in America any man or woman through hard work can achieve a life far better than in any other place in the world. We have a lot to be thankful for, and going to Africa really made me realize it.

13

TOP WHITETAIL HUNTS

I am often asked, what is my favorite animal to hunt? And while I really truly love to hunt all game, I guess if I had to pick one animal it would be either turkeys or whitetails. Don't ask me to go any deeper than that, as I don't know what I would pick if I could only have one of them. But if you ask me what is my favorite four-legged game to hunt, whitetails definitely get my vote.

Without a shadow of a doubt, whitetail hunting has always been and always will be one of my biggest passions, mainly because North America holds so many of them in such a wide variety of terrain. What I also like about them is that I think of whitetails as the everyday sportsman's game animal. In other words, they are accessible to everyone, they are not something out of reach. This is why everything in this industry hubs around the hunter's passion to pursue whitetails. I am no different from the everyday sportsman. When it comes to hunting whitetails, I am right smack in the middle of them. I'm driven by the same things that make other people watch shows on big whitetails. Having had the opportunity to hunt some of the places I have hunted over the years makes it easy for me to make a list of some of my top whitetail hunts. Some of them are memorable because of the size of the deer, while others are memorable because of the experience I had in the field.

It's important to recognize both things—sure, it's great to kill a really big buck, but size ain't everything. There is a bit of a split between traditional bowhunters and the younger hunters today. I really don't know how relevant Pope and Young is to our current hunting culture. Obviously any organization that promotes bowhunting and celebrates hunting in general is a good organization, but it is just my personal opinion that they really don't represent the modern bowhunter very well. At least they don't represent me and my friends who hunt. I don't know how important official recognition is to most bowhunters of my generation. I know it is not important to me personally. I have probably shot over forty "Pope and Young–class animals"—none of which are really Pope and Young because I never took the time to have them officially scored or entered. It just doesn't matter to me. I use their scoring system as a benchmark to judge a deer by, but I am not overly caught up by it. I consistently use gross score to describe a deer—a practice the Pope and Young Club is very much against. Their whole system is based on their idea of a "perfect" deer, which I think is a bit presumptuous to try and define. Anything less than perfect in their eyes is a deduction, and I don't think that way. The way I figure, it took that buck just as long to grow that kicker point, which may be a "deduction" in the club's eyes, as he did that "perfect" G2, so why not give him credit for it? But that's their club; they have every right to determine what criteria they want to promote to be part of the club. Just like I could start a "Longest Brow Tine Club" where we only let in deer with brow tines over ten inches. That would be our club's prerogative.

I think the biggest problem with Pope and Young is a failure to adapt with the times. I mean, Pope and Young has consistently come out against advancements in archery or modifications of techniques, whether that would be high let-off bows, electronic equipment mounted on bows, or crossbows. I have always been about including everyone I can in the celebration of this great sport, not excluding them because their bow has too much let-off or they use a battery-powered, lighted nock. It just doesn't make sense to me. In these times of dwindling hunter numbers, we need every ally we can get. Let me share some whitetail stories to show why we all do what we do.

THE NARROW MILK RIVER BUCK

One memory in particular comes from a deer I shot in Montana that we had been hunting for several weeks. I had been there as a cameraman, but I also arrived at camp early as I was going to be guiding a bit for various Realtree clients. In order to be prepared, I had spent some serious time getting to know the land and animals along that section of the Milk River. I had found several really nice bucks. So when the hunting season finally started, we brought in several prominent clients and professionals to hunt, such as noted whitetail assassins Greg Miller and Eddie Salter. The first evening they got there, we took them up to some of the high vantage points to glass and show them some of the deer we had scouted out. There were several really nice bucks inhabiting that stretch of the Milk River that they were interested in, but there was one deer I had found that really intrigued me, and I had been seeing him every night. He wasn't wide at all, only about thirteen inches, but he appeared to be heavy and tall even from the long distances I was glassing him. Because of his narrow frame, he really didn't look that impressive, though, compared to the other bucks we had scouted. But even from a mile away, when he would walk out onto the field, you could clearly see that he was a big, old-bodied deer, even if his rack was narrow.

Since he wasn't super-wide, nobody really paid a lot of attention to him, and nobody wanted to go hunt him even though he was coming out as regular as could be to this field. He was feeding in the northwest corner of the field we called "the Winke field," because outdoor writer and whitetail expert Bill Winke had killed a couple of really nice bucks there in years past.

At that time in my career, the program was, as our first priority, to get film of the guests hunting, and later, when one of them tagged out and a cameraman became available, I would get a chance to hunt. We had several guests in camp, and several cameramen, but I couldn't predict how soon I would get to hunt. Well, to my good fortune, on the first afternoon, three of our guests had killed deer, which freed up three cameramen. Now I could hunt.

Immediately I thought of going after that narrow buck. He was predictable, he was old, and he was heavy. When I saw him up close I might change my mind about him, but to start my hunt I first wanted to see how he looked from 35 yards.

On the first day, we couldn't go after him because the wind was wrong, so we decided to go hunt down in another area of the Milk River. That day I saw a couple of nice Pope and Young–class bucks, but they weren't so impressive that I had to release an arrow, so I let them walk. I still wanted to go see this narrow buck up close. The next day the wind shifted, coming perfectly out of the northwest, which would put the wind directly into our face so we could hunt the Winke field. We decided to take a gamble and hang a stand on a really small tree on the edge of the field. The tree was so small we could only get about eight or ten feet off the ground, but it was in the right spot. To give you an idea of how small this tree was, I couldn't even hunt standing up because we couldn't separate the two stands far enough apart. Typically, when filming a hunt, the cameraman will have a stand a couple of feet above the head (when standing up) of the shooter, essentially viewing over his shoulder. In this situation, the camera stand was just slightly above mine, so if I stood up to take a shot, I'd be blocking the camera's view. Not an ideal situation, but it was the best we could do under the circumstances.

We weren't there very long and had just got settled in when a few decent bucks came through, which bolstered my confidence about the setup. Then, as if he had read the script, here comes the narrow buck. The first thing I noticed about him was that his body, while it looked big from afar, was simply huge up close. He looked to be at least 300 pounds on the hoof, just a classic big-bodied northwest whitetail. While he was coming right for us, the way he was coming he could take a 20-yard trail, a 30-yard trail, or a 40-yard trail past our stand. Well, of course you know what he did . . . he took the furthest trail away from us. Like so often occurs with early-season deer heading to a food source, when he started getting close to the field he broke into a trot. I don't know if they do this out of anticipation of food, or fear of being out in the open and vulnerable, or what, but it is a common occurrence. I knew I had to stop him before I shot, so I came to full draw, and grunted really loud. He stopped instantly. Every muscle in his body was twitching, ready for flight. He was looking right at the base of my tree and even though I was only eight or so feet off the ground, he didn't have me pegged—yet. Without any hesitation, I centered my 40-yard pin and let the arrow go. Even though he was jacked up, he never moved and the arrow hit him perfectly.

It went in real tight behind the shoulder and hit off the shoulder blade and popped back out. When the arrow came out, my first thought was that I didn't get good enough penetration, but as he took off running, I could see the blood pumping out of him. I watched him until he disappeared and I felt certain he was down. I was amazed; it happened so fast it seemed surreal. We got down out of the tree, went over to where I last saw him, and found him down, right there. He looked even bigger on the ground than he did alive. When I got a hold of his antlers, he was exactly thirteen inches wide, but his body size made the antlers seem deceivingly small. In truth they were huge, heavy antlers, far better than anyone, including myself, had imagined. He ended up scoring 161 inches and was my best buck up to that time.

When I got back to camp, everybody's jaw just dropped when they saw this deer. It was sort of ironic, he turned out to be the best buck taken in camp, and he was probably the easiest to hunt. Everybody had the opportunity to hunt this deer, if they had wanted to. He was one of the more regular deer coming into the fields. It was early October, so he was feeding on alfalfa, and every day you could find him feeding in the same spot and using the same trails morning and night, but nobody wanted to hunt him because he just didn't seem that big in the spotting scope. It only goes to show you that sometimes you have to get up close and personal with a buck to really see how big he is.

This buck remains one of my favorites, not only because of his size, but because of all the time I spent scouting him and watching him. To put in that much effort, then to have your plan come together—it makes for a memory of a lifetime.

THE KANSAS GIANT

Another deer that means a lot to me is a big buck I killed in Kansas. I was hunting with Mike McKinsey. Bill Jordan was also in camp, which was a neat opportunity for me. I have always enjoyed hunting around Bill, so that made the place extra special. The camp itself was a small, quaint place back on the river bottom that just had a neat feel to it. While the camp was cool, the hunting promised to be even better, as there were deer just running everywhere. It was prime pre-rut conditions, right around the first week in November.

But while we were seeing lots of deer, we were not seeing lots of bucks. I had decided to use a buck decoy on this trip, because this river bottom was so open that the deer could see a long ways. My thought was if I could get a deer cruising through looking for does, hopefully I could grunt or snort-wheeze to him and maybe get him aggravated enough to try to run this particular deer (my decoy) out of the area.

There were lots of good stand sites all along the river bottom, but every day I hunted this one particular area. I liked this spot because it held a lot of deer. It had good bedding cover on one side, and there was a good food source just to the north of me. I was right in the middle, a prime spot to be any time you are whitetail hunting, regardless of region. Since I felt confident about this spot, I decided that I was going to work it every day until something convinced me I needed to hunt somewhere else.

On the third day of my hunt I woke up and could just feel that it was going to be one of those magical mornings. Up until then it had been warm, but now the weather had changed. The thermometer read 27 degrees and you could hear a pin drop it was so still. There was hard frost on the ground and the crispness in the air was almost palpable. One thing I have almost always found to be true is that when these conditions are present and are combined with rut or pre-rut activity, it's the optimal situation for deer movement.

I have also found that mornings are the most productive, providing the most opportunities when the pre-rut is in full swing. Deer are running and gallivanting all night and it carries over into the morning. So on this third morning, Mike McKinsey and I climbed up into the stands full of anticipation. It wasn't long before we knew our hunch was correct. Over the previous couple of days we had been doing some rattling without a lot of luck, but this morning it seemed that every time you touched the tines together a buck would emerge. Within the first couple of hours we had probably rattled in four or five small bucks. Then we rattled in one deer that was probably close to Pope and Young minimums, but the morning was so productive, I knew there had to be a huge deer around somewhere, and I let him walk. After we sat there for three or four hours the action started to slow down. In a whisper, I was quietly talking to Mike, recapping the awesome morning. Even though the action was tapering off, we were both still keyed up from all the activity, and we kept a watchful eye all around us. All of a sudden we heard this very audible grunt—and it was close. I mean, it was LOUD, son! There was no "Did you hear that?" sort of whispering over that one.

Mike immediately fired up the camera and I turned around to look over my shoulder for this buck. All I saw were these G2s charging down the trail. This buck had his ears laid back and he was ready to just stomp my decoy to smithereens. This joker was about 40 yards out, coming as hard as he could. I couldn't believe he had slipped up on us like that. All of a sudden, before I realized it, he was within 25 yards. I snatched my Hoyt from the Easy Hanger and drew back and grunted.

The buck stopped and I zipped him. The arrow hit him tight behind the shoulder and blew through the other side. He jumped, and took off at a dead run. Then my heart started trip-hammering. I hadn't even had that much time to look at him. All I knew was that he was a big-framed ole deer with long G2s. Big bucks are that way—you know with one look to kill them. You don't ever need to try and guess how big they are or field-judge them, you just instantly know they are big enough.

Well, when the arrow caught him he was broadside, and I knew he was a dead deer. He took off on a run, jumped the fence, and then stopped. He turned around, glared at that decoy, bristled up like he was going to fight—and dropped over dead. My heart was pounding. I knew he was a good deer, with a solid framed rack, with what I thought were eight points, but I didn't really know how good he was. We shakily got out of our stands and walked over there. It turned out he was actually a ten-pointer and scored 162 inches! This was just a stud of a deer. This deer was now my top-scoring whitetail, but he was much more than just a high-scoring deer. He makes my personal-favorites list because I got to go back and share the story with

Bill Jordan, and on top of that we had a good hunt on video. That buck later made the *Monster Bucks* series and a *Road Trips* episode. All in all, it was a very magical hunt that I won't soon forget.

OLD-SCHOOL KUDZU BUCK

Another favorite whitetail of mine was not a high-scoring deer at all, but he was a special buck all the same. This hunt took place when I was much younger, just getting involved in the outdoor industry. My brother-in-law, Shane Collier, and I had been hunting some local ground around our homes in Georgia. While we had several great hunting spots, we had been spending a lot of time scouting this big kudzu field and had a few nice bucks pinned down in it. In the early season, the deer down here just love eating kudzu. This plant, if you're not familiar with it, is kind of like a soybean leafy plant mixed with a sort of a vine. In fact, a lot of landowners used to plant kudzu around their homes, as it is similar to ivy in that it will grow up on the building, shading the house from the hot Georgia sun. Well, a lot of these old places became abandoned over the years through folks moving to the cities, and farms joining together to form larger corporate farms, but the kudzu stayed. So in our neck of the woods along the field edges and roads there are these large kudzu fields. You can't really get rid of it since it is so tough and hardy and spreads like wildfire. All that being said, it makes excellent early season whitetail forage.

Like I said, we had several good spots in the woods and on family farms to hunt, but we knew this kudzu field was going to be our number-one area any time the wind was right, 'cause we had these deer patterned. There was a bedding area to the south of there, so we knew where these deer were bedding and where they were feeding. We had seen three bucks in this group that we figured would be in the 120s to 130s, which are nice bucks for Georgia.

This was one of the first times that we had started trying to tape some of our hunts. We had bought us a VHS video recorder and our plan was to take turns filming each other.

Since it was kind of my brother-in-law's spot we had decided that he was going to hunt for the first day and a half and I would film him, then he was going to film me for a day and a half, and so on. We had three different two-person stand sites set up on this kudzu field, so for both Saturday and Sunday morning we hunted what we called the "kudzu stand," which was the closest stand to the field. It was only about 100 to 150 yards off the field. The first day proved fruitless, but on Sunday morning we got there well before daylight, and I mean WELL before daylight. In our youthful excitement, we got there like an hour before we could even think about shooting. Still, it wasn't very long after we got up in the stand and got settled down that we could hear these deer coming. It was still pitch-black dark, but you could make out their bodies when they got close. And, boy, did they ever get close; they picked a trail that took them directly under the stand. They literally walked right up under our stand, within feet of our position. Even in the darkness we could tell they were three bucks, probably the ones we had been seeing. We were amazed, as it was still dark and they were already heading back to their bedding area! Well, we were excited by the encounter, but a little disappointed, too, since we didn't even get a shot. It was unfortunate that Shane didn't get a chance to take a shot, because that afternoon was going to be my turn, with Shane filming me. That afternoon I was still pondering whether I should hunt as planned or let Shane have another crack at them when Shane ended my dilemma by saying, "Listen, man, fair is fair. It's your turn, get up there and hunt and I'll film you."

So we got set up, and it wasn't but two hours into our set that evening when some does came through. We let them walk, which was really out of character for Shane and me back then. We were slick-head killing machines at that time in our lives, no doubt about it. We liked to kill stuff, especially does, so letting them walk was a tough thing to do. They were big does, too, Boone and Crockett–level Georgia does, which made it even tougher. As it started getting closer to dark, we heard footsteps and we looked up and saw a pretty good-racked deer. It was hard to tell how big the rack was, as he was coming through some thick stuff, but judging by the direction he was taking, he was going to pass this one little hole where I might have an opportunity. It was going to be about a 30-yard shot. I got ready and drew back, and when he hit the hole, I released and just hammered this deer. He kicked, jumped, and ran off—I was some kind of pumped! Forcing ourselves to wait before blood-trailing him, we rewound the footage and discovered he was actually that ten-pointer, around 120 or 125 inches, that we had been seeing. So I was jacked up over this buck. Before we went to go find him, I said, "Let's go back and get my dad, I want him to see this deer." So we came back in with my dad and videoed the recovery of this buck. He turned out to be a nice buck that scored around 120 inches, but he field-dressed at 176 pounds, which is huge by Georgia standards. This buck later won the heaviest-deer contest that year, which netted me a gun and some cash— quite a treat for this country boy from Georgia.

What made this deer so special to me was it was one of the few bucks I got on camera before I started working for Realtree. To figure this deer out through scouting, then put him on the ground with a bow, and catch him on camera, all in my home state of Georgia, added up to a great deer hunt shared with a great friend.

THE HUNTRESS'S BUCK

One of the whitetails that means the most to me wasn't even my buck but my wife's. Ashley doesn't consider herself a professional hunter. She doesn't consider herself a Tiffany Lakosky or a Kandi Kisky or a Vicki Cianciarulo—she is not a woman who wants to make it in the hunting industry. She is a lady who has been very good to me and supports my hunting habits and understands my disease, when it comes to all manners of hunting, but she is not equally torn up about it. But because of my profession, I have had the opportunity to take her on some of her first hunts and be there when she killed her first whitetail and her first turkey, as well as on several duck and dove hunts. So through our relationship she has gotten involved in the outdoors and has learned to appreciate and even enjoy hunting, but she is not someone who is going to persevere through 10-degree weather, or hunt every morning, or get up two hours before light to hang stands, or trench through snow to get to a remote stand—that just ain't her. She is a laid-back evening hunter who loves hunting in the warm country of south Texas.

So one year I took her to Vatoville, Texas. Vatoville is a place that is full of 120- to 130-inch whitetails. We were happy with that. We went there just to go have fun and kill a mature deer. A big eight-pointer would be great, but really any old mature deer would have been fine as long as Ashley had a good time, and I thought we could get video of it, too. We weren't being picky.

So, the first evening, the Waddell family was sitting in the blind, enjoying the nice Texas weather. I was filming, Ashley was hunting, and my little boy Mason (who was only three years old) was sound asleep on the ground. After only two hours in the blind, Ashley turned to me and, out of the blue, said, "You know what? I want to shoot a deer like Tiffany or Kandi. I am tired of just trying to shoot a doe or a hog or maybe a little eight-pointer."

I was a little shocked, but I could tell all this was in good-natured fun. So I told her how she has to put her time in and work for it. Tiffany and Kandi definitely put their time in. I continued: "You're just hunting in the evenings, in places like Texas or Georgia, on little food plots—places that are easy to access, in weather that's nice. So you really don't deserve a deer like that, 'cause you have got to pay your dues."

So she continued whining and complaining and telling me that if I was such a great professional hunter then I would put her in a good spot where she could indeed kill a good deer, even if she only hunted Texas and Georgia in the evenings. By her reasoning, if she was a client and I was her guide, then I should try and find out a way for her to get one, regardless of how and where she wanted to hunt. So we were laughin' and cuttin' up, having this funny, half-serious, half-kidding conversation and not really paying much attention outside the blind.

Suddenly I caught movement out of the blind window and spotted a doe coming through the brush. I interrupted her and hissed, "There's a doe, Ashley," but she just continued talking, "Well, I have seen the deer that Tiffany shoots around the country—why can't I get a deer like that? I think if I was in the right spot, I know I could pull it off . . ." While she is still talking away, I look past the doe and out steps a big, huge, south Texas buck—way bigger than any other I had ever seen at Vatoville. I automatically switched to "go time" and calmly said, "Ashley, hush your mouth and get your gun, you're about to get your chance to shoot a deer like Tiffany and Kandi."

So she turns and glances back and sees this huge ten-pointer standing there and absolutely freaks out, losing her mind, and says several choice words that her dad would not be proud of her for saying. The buck is following that doe, and while I am preoccupied getting the camera fired up and on this buck, Ashley is just coming completely unhinged. Less than two minutes after I first saw this deer, he is now broadside at 100 yards. Ashley is hunting with a T/C Encore in .243 Winchester and has it trained on this deer. "Take your time," I whispered. "Get your sights right, squeeze the trigger, and make the shot." About then the gun goes off and the buck flinches. He runs off, and while we don't see him go down, I know she hit him good.

"Oh my gawd, what just happened?" Ashley gasped.

"I'll tell ya what just happened, you just killed a deer just like Tiffany or Kandi. Congratulations."

She walked up to that deer and literally cried. She was so excited, she almost felt undeserving. She felt bad about complaining how she never gets to shoot a big buck.

It just goes to show again that when hunting whitetails, luck counts for a lot. I have always felt that the best whitetail hunters are those who maybe don't necessarily know everything there is to know about whitetails, but they get out there and persevere. They spend their time in the woods, and when they get that rare opportunity on a deer they want, they close the coffin. Ashley hadn't done the first two things. She has not been someone who has persevered. She has not been someone who spends a lot of time in the woods or does a bunch of research, like scouting and reading topo maps. But she had done the last thing, which is just as important. When she got one good chance at a big whitetail, no excuses needed to be made—she pulled herself together and simply put the hammer down and killed him.

That buck ranks up there as one of my top hunts. He scored an awesome 154 inches and change, but much more important to me than his size was that Ashley was ecstatic, and my son Mason was there (even though he slept through the whole encounter, including snoring right through the shot). It is this kind of experience spent with your family that makes a buck rank really high in my book.

THE KANSAS WIND STORM

While I have a pile of great memories of whitetails stemming back all the way to my boyhood days, it is going to be hard to top the last couple of years I have had in the whitetail woods as far as sheer size goes.

The first memorable recent buck was in Kansas, with McMillan Outfitting. We were hunting out there with Blake Shelton, Miranda Lambert, Travis "T-Bone" Turner, and Nick Mundt, along with the whole *Bone Collector* crew of Steve Finch and Mark Womack. The year before I hunted out here for seven or eight days and never even came to full draw on a Pope and Young buck. But I had a feeling that sooner or later this place would give up a big buck—I just didn't know it was going to be my biggest buck to date.

From the very beginning, the hunt started off right, heating up pretty quickly. On the second day, Blake hunted a stand I hunted the day before and, like the assassin he is, killed a great deer in the 150-class range out of it. Not to be outdone, Nick also killed a good buck that night.

So I was hunting this area where I had been getting some good photos from my Bushnell Trail Scout camera of this really nice buck. From the photos this buck looked like a typical big eight-pointer with a little kicker off his main beam. We all guessed him around 155 or so. Definitely a nice buck; not one of the biggest I had ever killed, but a good one all the same, and one that I'd be happy to chase anytime. So I hunted this buck for four days straight and never saw hide nor hair of him.

Finally, on the fifth morning we were setting there and at about nine thirty or ten o'clock the wind started blowing so hard that I told the cameraman, "There is no way I could even take a shot at a deer if he is past about five yards." The wind was gusting between thirty and forty miles per hour, blowing my bow almost off the hanger. It was so bad we were even nervous to be sitting up in the stand. It was legal to put out some bait or attractant, so I had dusted the area around my stand with C'mere Deer that morning. But I had yet to have a deer come by and feed on it—mainly because I hadn't even seen a deer that morning. All of a sudden I spotted movement. A fawn popped out beside me about 20 yards away and walked through on the trail I was overlooking. Well, lo and behold, this fawn catches the scent of some of the C'mere Deer and immediately stops and starts licking the leaves. The fawn then starts nosing around, very intrigued by this scent that is in the air—it must be like having filet mignon sprinkled around for guys like myself and T-Bone. I was watching this deer for ten or fifteen minutes when I caught more movement from my right and all of a sudden here comes this buck we had seen on the trail cameras. He walked by my stand at 15 yards, but the wind was blowing so hard, I couldn't hold the pin on the deer. I finally settled it down enough to get a shot and was about to squeeze off when a wind gust pounded me so hard that it cranked the bow nearly back around behind my head. I took a breath, lowered the draw, and put the bow back down. Recomposed, I drew again and quickly got the pin on this buck and punched the trigger in between gusts. Luckily the arrow flew true and the range was close enough that it just smoked him. He was quartering away slightly when the arrow went in, and it blew out the other shoulder. The buck took off running and made it about 150 yards before toppling over. We finally got out of the tree and got over to the deer and I was just ecstatic when I realized he was way bigger than I thought he was. When we finally put the tape on him back at camp he ended up scoring 166 inches! He was an absolute giant of a deer. This was a monster typical mainframe deer; had he been a ten-pointer he would have made Boone and Crockett with ease. It was one of those deer that you have to hold in your hands to fully appreciate its size and mass. I knew this area would produce a good buck for me eventually; I was just amazed to realize it produced my biggest buck to date.

THE HOOSIER STATE MONSTER

Little did I know, though, that the following week would bring me a buck that would surpass even the Kansas buck in size. A week later I was headed for

Indiana, to hunt with the two brothers Al and Chris Collins. They are good friends with Scott Schultz and the Scent Blocker crew. They hosted myself and the *Bone Collector* team, as well as the cameraman Phillip Culpepper from *Road Trips*. I was there filming an episode for *Road Trips*, and the *Bone Collector* guys were filming an episode for one of their upcoming shows, which I was also going to appear on.

I had hunted at this place before and so I was amazed when Chris Collins said to me the first night, "Look, Michael, I don't know if you know this, but the buck that you saw last time you were here two years ago is still here." That got me pumped, since the buck he was talking about, and which I almost got a shot at two years prior, was in the high 140s to low 150s last I saw of him. Now with two more years under his belt, I couldn't wait to get a look at him—I could only imagine what two more years had done to his rack. Chris had seen him this season and guessed him between 160 and 170 inches. I could barely sleep I was so excited.

Once I knew this buck was still on the property, it was like I had tunnel vision. I wanted a crack at him. By the fourth day on the hunt we had seen this deer twice from the stand, and he looked every bit as big as Chris had described. We knew he was there, now

I was just excited to get an opportunity to get a shot at him. Two different times I had this deer dead to rights through rattling and the snort wheeze, but the wind caught us both times and spooked him off. Even though he would be tougher to hunt now that he had been spooked, we figured out he was living in this one particular area of the farm, which, ironically, was only 100 to 150 yards away from where I had seen him two years earlier. We were hunting between the second and third week of November and the rut was in full swing and quite evident as the deer were chasing hard.

We had been hunting mornings and evenings, and taking a break for lunch, but on the fourth day we decided we were going to sit all day. The deer were moving, we had seen this buck twice, and sitting all day just seemed like the right thing to do. At least it seemed like a good idea at first. But by about eleven in the morning I started rethinking that decision. Now, after sitting all morning, it seemed like a really bad idea. This particular morning was severely cold, and it had been snowing all day. Phillip and I hadn't seen any deer, and now we were ready to head back to the lodge to regroup. We were freezing cold, and we hadn't brought enough food to snack on—we were just plain miserable. Finally, around eleven thirty, I couldn't stand it anymore, so I texted Al and said, "Hey man, give us another hour or so then come get us. We need to get something hot to eat then we will come back for the evening hunt."

Just after I texted him I heard a twig break and I looked to my left and saw a doe, then a second, and then a third doe. After a couple of minutes the group grew to five does, which is a pretty good wad of deer even for this area of Indiana, which has a high deer population. Well, these deer were nonchalantly coming our way through the brush, but even though they appeared calm, the last one kept looking back behind her. I thought, "Please, please let there be a buck behind them." And sure enough another deer popped out and it was a buck. When I got a little better look at his rack, it was easy to see that it was a shooter buck. Another second passed, and when I finally got an even better look at him, I realized it was *my deer*. Here was the buck I had been trying to find for the last four days, and had been dreaming about for the past two seasons. The group of deer was about 55 to 60 yards away, working through this edge of thick woods. I didn't have a shot, so I decided to snort-wheeze at this buck. Now, I have never had much luck at getting a buck to come away from a doe with a snort wheeze or a grunt call, or anything, for that matter. But as soon as I did the snort wheeze, this buck pinned his ears back and started walking toward me. He got to about 50 yards before stopping. He turned around and headed back to the does. While the snort wheeze got his attention, it didn't make him commit. Having nothing to lose, I snort-wheezed again and the good Lord must have been looking down on me, or maybe this buck just had a terrible attitude about other bucks in his area, for he turned and started walking right to us. He was coming on a string, but was slightly downwind of us. I ranged a log that would intercept the path I figured he would have to come by. It was 37 yards away. Taking my time, I drew back, settled my pin, and waited. After what seemed an eternity, he finally got to the log. There was a small tree in the way of his vitals, but when he stepped around the tree, I had a clear shot. Applying pressure to the trigger, I sent the arrow on its way. At the sound of the bow, he started to crouch down to take off running, but he wasn't quick enough and the arrow slammed into him. The arrow caught him higher than I was aiming, but it also got his spine, which broke him down right on the spot. I couldn't believe it, there was no doubt that this was my new biggest buck ever. My hands were shaking as I wrapped my fingers around his massive antlers. Two years in the making, it was worth every second I had to wait. We scored him and he taped out at 174 inches (for fun we later rescored him and he scored 176). He was just a huge buck with 12 or 13 scorable points. He was a Hoosier state monarch. Tooth-aging proved he was six and a half years old, truly an old buck well into his prime.

I have been very fortunate to hunt whitetails a considerable amount. I have hunted them in many states and into Canada and I don't think I will ever get tired of hunting them. They provide me with the ultimate rush and often the hardest challenge. And while I have listed some of my most memorable hunts, to do so is a bit misleading, as every whitetail I have ever shot ranks up there as one of my top whitetails for one reason or another. As I have previously stated, some are memorable because of their size, some stick in the mind because of the challenge they present, while others are simply reminders of great times I spent in the field with friends and loved ones. I have found that because every whitetail hunting experience is so cool, every arrow, bullet, or sabot I shoot that hits true proves to be an opportunity for a great emotional experience, making for a pile of whitetail memories, and promising more in the future.

14

BOWS AND 'BOUS

Caribou weren't really something I dreamed about in my youth like I did elk, and to a lesser degree, moose. But as I got involved in the hunting industry and started watching more hunting videos, I started getting a hankering to chase caribou. Some of my earliest information about caribou came from Bob Foulkrod back in those early years when I was editing for Realtree Productions and Bob would send in this raw footage from the North. I saw on tape just how fun hunting caribou could be. In addition, caribou hunting looked like it offered plenty of challenges, especially if done with a bow and arrow. To top off the fun and the challenge, when I started seeing footage of that raw wilderness, I was captivated. I have always been mesmerized by solitary places, and the entire range of the caribou, from Alaska to Newfoundland, fits that bill pretty nicely. Thousands of animals, vast tracts of wilderness, and multiple tags to fill. I knew I had to make at least one trip to the tundra. Little did I know that one trip would never be enough.

The opportunity to be in the middle of nowhere with bow in hand and lots of targets nearby gets any bowhunter excited. The excitement and passion of hunting the North is compounded by the country itself. I love it. It is the kind of place where you just don't run down the road to the nearest hardware store and pick up supplies if you run out of something. Everything has to be well planned. Everything from gear to grub to fuel to soda pop is a challenge to get into caribou camp and is typically hauled in either by plane or by boat. You don't realize how remote you are until you start thinking about the cost of airplane fuel per gallon and calculating how many single cans of Coke can be crammed in a small bush plane.

It would be several years after my work with Bob Foulkrod before I'd have the opportunity to take a crack at caribou. The problem was simply one of economics and time. Even though caribou are one of the more affordable big-game species to hunt, they are still nowhere near as affordable as hunting whitetails and turkeys in the Lower 48. Since David Blanton was pretty budget conscious and wanted to make sure we got the best bang for our buck, we did a lot of stuff in the Lower 48, more often than not places we could drive to. Going on a caribou hunt was out of the question. Depending on where exactly we planned to hunt, it would take at least ten days from start to finish; we would have to fly north to the nearest major city and then hire a floatplane or a boat to get us into the backcountry. It all added up to a time-consuming and expensive trip.

However, the format of *Realtree Road Trips* gave me the premise to try some different things, one of which was caribou. The first chance to travel north and experience some of the wild tundra came via Ralph Cianciarulo, host of *Archer's Choice*. One day he called up and asked me if I wanted to go hunting. Always interested in hunting anything anywhere, I said sure, what did he have in mind? He wanted me to go to Quebec with him and his wife, Vicki, to hunt Quebec/Labrador barren-ground caribou. I couldn't have been more excited.

I needed to learn everything I could about caribou. After doing a bunch of research and talking with guys like Chuck Adams and Bob Foulkrod, I found out that caribou represented the best opportunity to kill a Pope and Young animal of any big-game species. While this was true of almost all types of caribou hunting, it was especially true in Quebec since there are so many caribou in the migration. The fact of getting an animal "in the books" really wasn't that important to me, but I have to admit I did like the idea of an animal with all that bone on top of their head.

So we worked through the details and spent the following year planning the trip. I was going to do it for *Realtree Road Trips*, with Steve Finch doing the filming and field producing. Ralph and Vicki were doing it for their own TV show. I was really starting to look forward to this trip. I was excited to get close to one of these trophies of the North, just as I was excited to see the rugged northern country, and on top of that I was pretty happy with how the crew was shaking up. Steve is always fun to travel with, and Ralph and Vicki were going to be a treat in camp.

If you don't know Ralph and Vicki, walk up to them at a sports show and say hi, you won't be disappointed. They are truly good people. I had always looked up to them as they are such classy folks, and they have accomplished so much through hard work and perseverance. They are super down-to-earth and have remained the same regardless of what opportunities they have received through the hunting industry. These folks are as rooted as they come. They just love to hunt and are dang good at it.

One thing unique about this hunt was that Steve Finch was going to get a chance at hunting as well as running the camera. The plan was I would shoot one and Steve would film, and then he would shoot one and I would film him. I brought my bow, and also a Thompson/Center muzzleloader, just in case we needed to use that. As a side note, Steve is very creative and extremely talented, but sometimes he can be kinda scatterbrained. In the process of getting ready to go, he got a new Hoyt bow and Beman arrows, and everything was all set up and ready to go. Well, in the process of getting up there, his bow got either lost or stolen (we still aren't sure to this day), and he had two different sets of Beman arrows get either lost or stolen. It took some frantic phone calls, but we finally got him reoutfitted with all the gear he needed, never mind the fact that Hoyt nearly went broke in the process.

We finally got to camp and I immediately realized what makes caribou hunting so cool. It is one of the few social big-game hunts. As anyone who knows me can tell ya, I am sort of a people person, I like to talk and hear stories and joke with my buddies. Unfortunately, on most deer or turkey hunts, you get up well before light and head your separate ways, not getting a chance to catch up until you rendezvous at camp that night. Combine this with the fact that hunting is kind of slow, such that many hunters aren't in that good of a mood. Caribou hunting is just the opposite from this. It is much more like a duck or a bird hunt, where the hunters are getting action, and they are relaxed, just having a good time, with no pressure. You can spot game as a group and one person can make the final stalk while the others watch. It really is the most social big-game hunt I have ever done—and I loved it. A typical day in a caribou camp involves getting up, eating a nice breakfast as it is cracking daylight, socializing around the camp a bit while waiting for the outfitters and guides to get the boats and gear ready, and then you strike off in small groups. Generally you will head to a higher vantage point and set up to glass. Once a good bull is spotted—or group of bulls, which is more often the case—you make a plan to either cut them off and set up an ambush, or, if they are staying still, to put a stalk on them. This type of hunting is much like the mule deer hunting of the West I love—you get a chance to formulate a plan with friends, then make it happen. There is really no downtime.

One thing I had heard before I went, and which I saw after I got there, is that you can be in them one day and they can be gone the next. This is simply a fact of hunting a migrating game species. I found that it's common practice for an outfitter up there to maintain multiple spike camps so they can monitor the migration and then use the camps that the caribou are going to intersect with. Most of the outfitters up there also offer at least one move. So if the camp they put you in isn't panning out, they'll move you to a new camp where the caribou are coming through.

For the first couple of days of my first Quebec caribou hunt we hunted right around the camp, as bulls had been moving through there in good numbers. But it soon became apparent that the numbers were drying up. Luckily we had an outfitter who was prepared to move us. So we decided to crank up the floatplane and make a move to another area. We moved down to a new chain of lakes where the outfitter thought the bulls would be heading. Immediately upon landing I was amazed at the number of caribou around this new spot. We went from not seeing many animals in the first camp to being in the middle of one of the wonders of the world—the caribou migration.

Until you have seen an animal migration of this magnitude, it is hard to imagine. I would guess the wildebeest migration across the Serengeti, or the old bison migration in the West, must be similar, but the caribou migration is the only thing I have ever seen of that magnitude in nature. Animals were everywhere. Bulls, cows, and calves were working their way south.

Feeding while on the move, they walked faster than any man could run across the same ground. They had trails literally beat through the tundra, with communal crossing points at the various lakes and rivers. From the air, you got the impression of looking down onto an anthill—they were literally running everywhere. Now, in most states in the U.S.A., you can't land a plane and hunt the same day—but Quebec is a different story. We landed the plane and I got my gear and started hunting almost immediately. It was probably nine thirty in the morning, and I quickly realized we were in a perfect spot. We were at the front end of the migration and there were thousands of animals to choose from, so I decided to hold off and be picky. Sitting behind a pile of rocks, I probably let between 200 and 300 bulls walk past well within range. The previous day, I would have been delighted to take any one of them, but there were simply so many animals to choose from now, so my standards had risen a notch even though I had never killed a caribou.

I wanted a double-shovel bull that would score well into Pope and Young, but even with so many to choose from, it wasn't that easy to find one with double shovels. They say less than 10 percent have double shovels. Finally I spotted the bull I was looking for. He was swimming across this lake and was about halfway across, so we ran to get up ahead of where he was likely to come out of the water. We got lucky. Even though it is somewhat predictable where a bull is going to come out of the water, it is never certain as there are so many different trails they can choose from. We took a guess and got situated behind some cover. Lo and behold, when that bull came out of the lake, shaking off his thick hair, he sauntered right past our hiding spot.

I drew back, waited for him to stop, and then realized: caribou seldom stop for a shot. I led him a slight bit and released the arrow. It hit true, right in his ribs, and he took off on his death run. While I am occasionally blessed with good luck, I also get my fair share of raw deals. That bull immediately ran over the hill, jumped into the lake, got a good distance offshore, and promptly died. I was completely dejected. The wind and current were combining to push him further offshore, and it was doubtful whether he would drift to any place we could readily reach. I took one look at the guide and Steve and made the decision right then and there that I wasn't going to let my first caribou drift away like that. Without a word, I stripped down to my underwear, swam out into this lake, grabbed my caribou, and swam back. It was freezing! The temperature was in the mid-thirties, and I don't believe the water was any warmer. I had never missed the warmth of

Georgia more. I think I almost got hypothermia, and nearly passed out from the cold, but in the end I got my caribou.

Now that I got my first bull out of the way, it was time to share the wealth. I grabbed the camera and Steve grabbed his Hoyt and we headed back out to see what was still around. We shouldn't have worried about the numbers of caribou left around this new camp as there were still plenty. Steve Finch went on to kill really nice bulls with his bow before I stuck the camera back in his hand and killed my final bull as well. Everything I had heard about caribou was spot on—when you're in them you're really in them.

While the hunting was phenomenal, what impressed me the most about caribou hunting was our complete and utter removal from civilization. I don't think we as a human race get enough of that. Now, I'm not talking about removal from camaraderie or conversation—we had plenty of that—but from the day-to-day hustle and bustle of modern life. In caribou camp it doesn't take long for the desolation to sink in and restore your soul. Having the unobstructed ability to unwind with your friends, simply watch the sunset, and know that you don't have to check your e-mail or answer the phone is a simple pleasure that few of us get to enjoy anymore. It is probably as close to being an old mountain man as most of us living in the modern world will ever get to experience. It is that type of isolation that really recharges your batteries. When caribou hunting, you can take ten days out of your life and ultimately become a grain of sand in the grand ocean of the world.

From a bowhunter's perspective, I found that chasing caribou gave me the opportunity to see lots of wildlife that doesn't see lots of people. It is not that caribou are inherently dumb, as some people seem to think. They are just naïve. They spend the majority of their lives in the wilderness, and, aside from the occasional wolf or bear, they don't run into predators that often, especially not the two-legged variety.

Since that first hunt in 2003, which aired on season one of *Road Trips*, I have had the opportunity to go back to Quebec two more times. I took one trip with Mirage Outfitters and one with Safari Nordik. Both of the hunts turned out to be unbelievable. Considering that we were literally at the end of the earth, not that far from the Arctic Circle, both had great camps, good food, and excellent equipment—none of which is easy to get up there. It is not like you can just run down to Home Depot and buy some plywood. Anything you bring into that area is a chore in itself. However, what I have found hunting caribou in several different locations with a few different outfitters—and I have heard this as well from trusted friends in the business—is that if you pick a big operation, most of the time you are going to have a good hunt. A legitimate caribou outfitter almost anywhere in the North is going to have multiple good camps.

I am occasionally asked by folks interested in going on their first caribou hunt whether it is better to go early or late in the season. While I am no expert, what I have found is that, apart from weather conditions (early can be hot and buggy, late can be super-cold and snowy), there really are three stages of any caribou hunt, and each offers its own challenges and styles of hunting. These three stages can happen regardless of what month you go, since outfitters are following the herd from the north to the south, from numerous different camps. I have hunted them before the main migration kicked in, right in the middle of the migration, when there were so many animals around it was hard to pick out a single bull to shoot, and even after the migration started to peter out and it was only solitary old bulls left. I have found that each of these situations is fun, but each is a bit different in its own way. Since you really have little control over exactly where you are going, and you have no control over the actual migration of the animals, all I can say is, don't overthink this part of the hunt, just be ready to adapt once you get there.

I can't stress this last point enough. Try to become as proficient as you can with a wide variety of hunting styles. If you only bowhunt out of trees, you are going to be at a severe disadvantage in the tundra, where there aren't many trees over six feet tall. Practice shooting from all positions, from sitting to kneeling to standing. Practice using your rangefinder instantly, and practice spotting and stalking game through broken country. I have hunted caribou several ways, including ambushing them, spotting and stalking them, and simply waiting for them like you would a whitetail. All forms have been challenging, but hunters must be prepared to adapt to the conditions.

It is usually not a very hard hunt, although it can be, if you really push yourself. But what I liked about it most was the chance of filling your tags nearly 100 percent of the time. Most hunters who are accustomed to hunting big-game species in the Lower 48 will appreciate the fact that caribou aren't overly spooky. They don't see a lot of people and don't get pressured much, so there are a lot of things you can get away with on caribou that you couldn't do with elk or whitetails. Keep this in mind when making a stalk. There have been many instances when I made a stalk across pretty open tundra that you would never get away with in the Lower 48. You can be very aggressive in your stalking. You can also get set up way ahead of time when they are migrating and they generally will stick to the same trail or path that the others followed.

Many places allow two caribou tags, and the opportunity to fill both of them is really pretty good. However, I would advise anyone who goes north for caribou to pick a quality outfitter, as it is big country out there. Yes, there are lots of animals, but there is even more country. If you miss the migration, you've got to have the ability to get relocated in front of them or you will find out just how lonely the tundra can be.

The hardest part of caribou hunting is knowing which animal to shoot. At first they all look huge, and most first-time hunters make the mistake of shooting an animal that isn't nearly as big as they wanted, just because at first they all look so good. While I'm no expert at scoring them, I have looked over literally thousands of caribou, and I can tell you that what you want to find is really pretty simple. You want to find one with good top points and good bottoms points, commonly referred to as the "bez" points. A big shovel is a plus, and two are better than one, though double shovels are rare.

In my opinion, caribou are the perfect game to chase as a group and are an ideal big-game animal for the bowhunter, as there are generally lots of opportunities to get that perfect shot. I always recommend to my friends that they get a group of buddies together and go on a caribou hunt. Get enough guys to take over a camp and it turns into a blast. It is so much fun to share in each other's success. With the right group of friends a caribou camp can be a magical experience.

15

SPEED GOATS

I have always thought antelope were cool animals. I am intrigued by them in large part because of how they live, not just where they live. In many ways antelope are similar to turkeys. They have great noses and good hearing, but they really use their phenomenal eyesight to alert them to danger and predators. They are one of the fastest animals in North America, earning them the nickname "speed goats." They use this speed to get them out of harm's way.

They are traditionally thought of as a rifleman's quarry. But for me, being tore up with the string-music affliction, I wanted—no, needed—to hunt them with the bow and arrow. I knew it would be a huge challenge to get within bow range with their jacked-up senses, let alone come to full draw, but it was something I had to try, even if it was just one time.

About the time the antelope bug hit me, we were in the middle of producing *Road Trips*, and I decided there was no better topic for the show. Anytime I get to go out West and hunt something different and spend some time with good friends, it always makes for a great *Road Trips* episode. So I called a buddy whom I really look up to and respect: Fred Eichler of Full Draw Outfitters. Many recognize Fred today from his job hosting Hoyt's wildly successful TV show, but not many folks know he started his hunting career and subsequent TV career as a successful outfitter, specializing in all things bowhunting.

Operating out of Trinidad, Colorado (known for two things: a big gunsmithing school and a hospital specializing in sex-change operations), he had been running successful camps for a long time. I decided that would be the perfect place to experience my first antelope hunt. Not only did I know there would be great hunting out there, but also I couldn't think of a better person to spend time with than Fred.

When I arrived out in Colorado, I really only had a little bit of knowledge about hunting antelope with a bow. I knew that it was traditionally done hunting over a water hole out of a blind. I also knew that they were very wary, and that I needed to be prepared to take longer shots than the average whitetail hunt required. Also, from my own experience hunting over water holes, I knew one other thing: the hotter and dryer the conditions, the better.

When cameraman Phillip Culpepper and I went out there, both of us were pretty much virgins to antelope hunting (apart from what we had seen on TV or read about or heard from other hunters), but right away we noticed something about Fred's area that impressed us—he kept it bowhunting only. As you can imagine, this makes a big difference in the wariness of animals. While the "bowhunting only" rule was a huge advantage for us, it was as if the hunting gods decided to bring the playing field back down to level. Wouldn't you know it, it was just our luck, right before we got there, that it rained. In all of the research I had done prior to this trip, one thing I distinctly remember reading was that antelope can literally drink out of a hoofprint and that will last them all day. The rain was a bad omen and I knew we were now going to be up for a real challenge.

The first day, Fred put us in an Ameristep blind. We were to set in it all day. As when using a blind anywhere, for any species, we wanted it as black as possible inside that blind to hide any movement should an antelope come in. So even though the temperature was hot, we kept the windows buttoned up and all the mesh up and the top closed. If the temperature at midday was sweltering outside, inside the blind it was even worse, reaching over 110 degrees. I felt like a biscuit in a southern oven in there—the heat was unbelievable!

It was a very frustrating day. By the time we crawled out of there at dark we were each probably fifteen pounds lighter. We were also a little depressed. We traveled all the way from Georgia to get there, then spent twelve to fifteen hours inside that oven-like blind, looking out across the vastness of the prairie and a water hole 50 yards away. Seeing antelope was not a problem—they were everywhere. But seeing them at 800 or 1,000 yards away when you have a bow in your hands, well, you might as well not be seeing them at all. There is nothing you can do.

That first day Phillip and I didn't bring anything to read. By noon we were absolutely bored out of our gourd with nothing to do, so we just sat there, staring across the plains. Occasionally you would see a dove or some small bird come in and drink, and once in a while you would see an antelope walk across the plains, but never would they come in. Like a mirage, they would just disappear back into the heat waves.

After the first day I was pretty aggravated. On day two, we went to the blind at daybreak, but this time I brought a book: *Fred Bear's Field Notes*. I actually read that book *twice* that day out of sheer boredom.

I can almost recite verbatim all of Fred's stories. But other than having some reading material, the second day went just like the first day.

After two days of this boredom my opinion was that antelope hunting ranks right up there with putting your ear in a rat trap. I remember sitting there one day and thinking, "Holy cow, this is insanely not fun." But I knew that if it had been really dry like it was supposed to be, the hunt would have been a lot more action packed.

On hunts like these, as I've come to realize over the years, you just have to keep a positive attitude and be patient. Sooner or later something will happen. We knew the animals were there, and we knew there were quality animals, as we had seen them from afar through binoculars. So we persevered.

We got more books, more water, and kept sitting in that blind. Finally, on the fourth day, right at daybreak, I saw a Pope and Young antelope walking toward us from way away. Before getting too close, he angled away a bit and bedded up, probably 500 yards from our blind. While not as good as coming all the way in for a drink, he was at least closer. Now we were starting to get excited. Since we arrived, there had been no rain, so most of the surface water had dried up, with the exception of our water hole, and now we had an antelope bedding within 500 yards of us. This setup was starting to look sort of promising. After about an hour of staring at this goat, however, our enthusiasm started to wane. Ten hours later, this animal still hadn't gotten out of his bed. Now we were getting dejected again. There was maybe an hour or so of shooting light left in the day before the sun met the horizon and the fourth day would close like all the previous ones had. However, before we completely gave up hope, off to our right I noticed a doe and a little yearling get up out of their bed and start walking toward us. As if on cue, the buck, watching the doe and yearling, followed suit, getting up out of his bed and sauntering in our direction.

"It's on," I whispered to Phillip. "We're gonna get this buck."

My heart was just pounding in my chest. When you wait for four days for something to happen, when it finally looks like it's all going to come together, the excitement and anticipation can be almost too much to handle.

Then I looked back and saw this doe and fawn turn away from us and walk straight out into the flats to feed, just like all the others had done in the past. The buck took one look at them, turned, and followed them out onto the flats.

"You have got to be kidding me!" I almost screamed. I had lost my religion by now, I was totally freaking out, swearing under my breath, claiming I was never coming antelope hunting again. I just couldn't believe our misfortune.

We were both furious, and complaining like a bunch of spoiled rotten young-uns without a pacifier. We were almost to the point of throwing my bow and his camera out of the blind window and walking home.

In the middle of my tantrum, however, I looked back out there and saw that buck stop, turn around, and make a beeline for our water hole. My complaining instantly stopped, my throat got dry, I had cottonmouth, and my heart was bursting out of my chest. "Oh my gawd, he's coming," I whispered to Phillip, who was already busy firing up the camera.

To this day I don't know if I have ever been any more nervous about the anticipation of a shot. We had put in our time, our emotions had taken a roller-coaster ride, and now we had an opportunity to pull it off—*that* is pressure.

He walked straight in. When he finally got to between 25 and 30 yards, I came to full draw. My heart was still beating out of my chest, but I managed to get the pin on the buck. He was quartering slightly to, but I put the pin on him, didn't hesitate, punched the trigger, and nailed him. He took off running like he was racing in the Talladega 500. Approaching turn one, he went into a spin and never recovered. After spinning around a few times, he finally picked up his parking ticket and died right there. I was some kind of elated— this emotional rush on the heels of four hot, long days was almost too much to handle.

We went out and looked at him and he was a great goat, especially for my first antelope. I looked down into my bag for my tag and I didn't see it. "Heck, I must have left it back at the lodge," I thought. No worries, I just wouldn't move him, and we had some filming to do anyway on the recovery. I would just have someone bring my tag out from the lodge when they came to pick us up. Well, about that time I look up and here comes a game warden's truck, driving out to pay us a visit.

After all the hours, days, and weeks I had spent in the field hunting, doing everything right and never seeing a game warden, this sure was a rotten time for one to pull up. Thinking it might be wise to take another look for this tag, I started rooting around in my hunting bag. Luckily, I found it in the bottom of my bag. As it turned out, the warden was really nice and celebrated the hunt with us and went on and on about how tight an operation Fred runs. It was the perfect ending to a tough, long, and mostly uneventful trip.

But what this trip did do for me is reinforce my belief in how much the situations surrounding the hunt can affect it. It can be the weather, like we experienced on this hunt. It can be other hunters' pressure. It can be the moon phase. It can just be the particular time of year. It is the extra circumstances that surround a hunt that make it tough or easy. Sometimes you will go to a place and all the conditions align and your hunt is a slam dunk. Other times, like with this hunt, because of a heavy rain before we arrived, it will be darn tough. And this situation was not typical. Most times this area of Colorado is bone dry and Fred's hunters have multiple opportunities to get the animal of their dreams—in fact they are wading through shot opportunities until the one they want appears. But our bad luck with the rain reinforced another valuable lesson: you have to have the skills to make hay when the sun shines. After four days of hunting, we had only one shot opportunity. You have to be ready to capitalize on that rare opportunity when it presents itself or you run a big risk of going home empty-handed. The good news is, it is this last part that you can do something about. A hunter can never control or predict the extra factors, but he can practice every day until he is comfortable making any reasonable shot opportunity.

Since that first hunt in Colorado I have had a chance to hunt antelope in a few different places—from Nevada to New Mexico to one really memorable hunt in Montana, where I was on a whitetail/elk/antelope hunt. As it turned out we were lucky enough that on the second day of our hunt we shot a really nice whitetail down in a river bottom, which gave me an opportunity to go chase some antelope. So, like in Colorado before, I went and sat in a blind overlooking a water hole.

There was another client in camp who had also been hunting deer and antelope, but he really wanted to kill a nice antelope. So he had been sitting at this one particular water hole for three days prior to my getting there. Turns out, it had been so hot and dry that he had passed out in the blind, basically falling over, hitting his head and cutting himself really badly. Passing out is a sign of a hot blind. It seems the temperature in that blind was reaching 120 degrees in the middle of the day. Well, the night before, this client told us, "There's no way I'm going back to that antelope blind, I've had enough of it. But somebody oughta go in there and hunt." So the outfitter told me and Phillip to get in there and hunt that blind as it was a good blind, and a good opportunity at a great buck. Although the client hadn't seen anything during his few days of vigil, the outfitter was convinced that sooner or later a bruiser that he had been seeing around would show up there. I looked at Phillip, and he looked at me, and we both had the same thought: "Oh no, here we go again. Another hot, boring antelope hunt."

Knowing that the other client had sat in the blind for several days prior without seeing anything didn't boost our confidence any. We both couldn't help but think, "How dumb is this! The last guy passed out because it was so hot, and now we are considering sitting there? Didn't we learn anything in Colorado?"

So we weren't real gung ho to get after it. We slept in a bit late, had a nice brunch (that's the meal between breakfast and lunch, for my Georgia buddies), and got to the blind around eleven o'clock. I was just relax-ing, wearing a short-sleeved T-shirt, not really taking the hunt too seriously, as really there was no pressure. We had already killed a good whitetail, about a 150-class animal, so the rest of the trip was just gravy. We were chillin' out, and talking a bit; I was almost get-ting ready to take a nap. I looked at my watch and it was about twelve thirty—and it was starting to get hot. So we kicked back, reflecting on the long day we had ahead of us. Both of us were half asleep, and neither of us was paying any attention, when all of a sudden I heard "click, click, click." I glanced out of the blind to see what the commotion was. It turned out to be hooves on hard dirt. There was a monster antelope strolling down to the water hole. I immediately got Phillip's attention and he got the camera rolling and caught this goat making his approach. I grabbed my Bushnell rangefinder and hit him with it; he was 33 yards away, standing broadside. In no time, I came to full draw, settled the pin, and put the smackdown on him—he ran up the hill and fell dead. It was that simple. I looked at my watch and we had been there exactly an hour and forty-five minutes. Still a bit in shock, we walked up to the big buck. I was amazed to see the mass of this animal. He ended up scoring around 76 inches.

It just goes to show you that once again, random luck can make all the difference in the world. For four days a guy suffered in that blind, and then we saunter in after a leisurely brunch, wait less than two hours, and put the smackdown on a big buck. Sometimes life just isn't fair, but if you wait long enough, you will get lucky once in a while.

Antelope hunting is a lot of fun. It can be unbelievably cool, and it is often done in some of the neatest country that you will ever get to hunt—but I think antelope rate up there in my top five of the most aggravating animals I have ever hunted with a bow. They have great vision, are hard to stalk, don't drink a lot, and even when everything is working in your favor, they seem to have a sixth sense about danger.

Will I hunt them again? Of course I will. I wouldn't miss it for the world.

Epilogue

You know, I have been around the world and have done many different things in the hunting industry, but I still have some destinations I want to see and hunt and will probably take the time to do so shortly. From all that I've heard, I suspect New Zealand is a target-rich environment for a bowhunter, so I probably need to pay those islands a visit with a quiver full of Eastons. Of course, going back to Alaska, even with all its hardships, would be a treat, especially if I can get to go after a big ole brown bear. I would like to shoot another moose with my bow; they are just too big not to want to shoot them again and again; and of course I would like to return to Africa to close the deal on a "black death" buff with a stick and string.

All that being said, after hunting exotic critters and traveling around the world a bit, I have realized I enjoy whitetail and turkey hunting just as much as ever, and they come with a lot less in the way of travel expenses. Oh, sure, I'll still go out West every year as I can't seem to get enough of the western landscape and the big ole critters that hang there, but for the most part I will probably be back in Booger Bottom, boosting one of my young-uns into the same old "corner stand" that I shot my first buck out of.

By introducing me to the outdoors, my father gave to me a lifestyle I never could have imagined, and I intend to do the same for my tribe of young-uns. I don't care whether they all take to hunting like I did or not, but I think they should at least have the opportunity to see if they like it, and at the very least they should understand what it's all about. I think that basic under-standing of nature and the natural way makes anyone a more balanced, well-rounded adult.

I have said it before and I will say it again. Hunting is something that transcends success, jobs, income, fame, and status. If my run in this industry ends tomorrow, I know one thing: I will still have a bow, a quiver full of arrows, and a hunting license, and at the end of the day that's all that matters. As long as I can climb up into an old tree stand overlooking a prime piece of Georgia river bottom with the hope that a freak nasty buck may stroll by, I will be content.